W9-CKI-891

# Ed Slott's RETIREMENT RESCUE!

The Exclusive Program Guide

By **Ed Slott**, CPA

Copyright © 2012

*Your Companion to the Public Television Special*

**Ed Slott's Retirement Rescue!**

## Disclaimer and Warning for Readers

This "Program Guide" companion to the "Ed Slott's Retirement
Rescue!" program and the related Bonus DVDs and CDs is a
commonsense approach to personal finance. In practical advice
programs, as in life, there are no guarantees, and users of this
guide are cautioned to rely on their own judgment about their
individual circumstances and to act accordingly. Users of this
Program Guide are also reminded that it is intended for
informational purposes only and is not meant to take the place
of professional advice. The laws in this area are complex and
constantly changing. You should consult with an experienced
professional to apply the relevant laws in your state to your
unique situation.

In addition, Ed Slott does not endorse, sell or advise on investments
or any financial products such as life insurance, annuities, mutual
funds, stocks, bonds or similar products and has limited knowledge
of these financial products. Ed Slott is also not a partner or owner
of any company that sells or advises on investment products like
the ones mentioned in the above sentence.

# Ed Slott's
# RETIREMENT RESCUE!

## The Exclusive Program Guide

### By **Ed Slott**, CPA

## TABLE OF CONTENT

# Ed Slott's RETIREMENT RESCUE!

## The Exclusive Program Guide

By **Ed Slott**, CPA

www.irahelp.com
Copyright © 2012

*Your Companion to the Public Television Special*

**Ed Slott's Retirement Rescue!**

And the **5** Bonus DVDs:

- ▸ **IRAs Are Different**
- ▸ **The Amazing Stretch IRA**
- ▸ **Life Insurance for Life and Beyond**
- ▸ **Critical Items for Critical Moments**
- ▸ **11 Ways to Supercharge Your Roth IRA**

And the **2** Bonus CDs:

- ▸ **Life Events**
- ▸ **Advisor Checkup**

# Ed Slott's RETIREMENT RESCUE!

## The Exclusive Program Guide

This Program Guide provides you with a recap of all of the major items covered on the Public Television Program *"Ed Slott's Retirement Rescue!"*

In addition, it includes a summary of the key points covered on the bonus DVDs, PLUS items not covered on the show or on the bonus DVDs, PLUS the key points of the material covered on the bonus CDs.

You can watch the program and the bonus DVDs and CDs, then use this guide to follow along. This will help you better understand, reinforce and remember the most important points. Then you can take action and create a plan to keep more of the money you make.

You've got a lot of information here. Now it's time to Rescue Your Retirement!

−Ed Slott

**Part**

**1**

**Key Points from Part One:**

**Big Message:** There are things that you can control and things that you cannot.

Focus on what you can control. Focusing on factors you cannot control builds anger, frustration, negativity and financial insecurity.

The good news:

If you focus on what you can control, the other negative issues will be less important and less overwhelming. You won't have to worry about your retirement security!

You can turn confusion into clarity by putting the financial jigsaw puzzle pieces together. I give you these pieces throughout the program and show you how to use them.

I call these pieces the **5 Silent Retirement Killers**

1. **Taxes**
2. **Risk**
3. **Saving Money**
4. **Uncertainty**
5. **Inactivity**

# PART ONE

Welcome to Retirement Rescue!

What's the best decision you have EVER made?

Getting married? Buying a home? Getting divorced? Selling your home? Getting re-married? Buying another home? Retiring?

Let's rephrase the question: What's the best ***FINANCIAL*** decision you have ever made?

For many of you, probably the biggest and best single financial decision of your life was way back when, when you decided to contribute to a retirement account—a 401(k) at work or an IRA, and continued that disciplined process ever since.

That one single financial decision has paid off… and that's why you have retirement money, so you deserve congratulations!

That one single financial decision really has paid off.

But you cannot just set it and forget it. Your retirement savings need to be protected and rescued.

I call it "Retirement Rescue" because your retirement savings are at high risk of being lost. I'm not talking about the stock market and other situations that we cannot control. I'm talking about things you CAN control and CAN do something about.

Do you ever plan on retiring? Every study says it's not possible and you'll probably have to work until you drop.

How's that sound?

It's depressing, but the good news is… it's not necessarily true.

Why?

Because the biggest roadblocks between you and your retirement savings are things you can control.

You can rescue your retirement!

So why is everyone saying we're doomed?

Because let's face it, most people focus on negative issues. You know you want to be the first one to tell everyone the bad news. We love to talk about other people's misery.

Someone sneezes in Europe and now you've lost your retirement savings. This is insane!

And when things seem out of our control we tend to give up, get depressed, get angry and do nothing… or worse, make horrible decisions.

That's certainly true when it comes to your retirement savings.

And it is upsetting. I'm certainly not minimizing the disaster our retirement savings have gone through. Lots of 401(k)s and IRAs are on life support after the financial meltdown caused by our "respected" financial institutions.

You have to feel betrayed — by the very institutions we are supposed to be able to trust with our money. You can't even say the words "trust" and "Wall Street" in the same sentence. People would laugh at you.

And these Wall Street titans are always claiming they are worth millions because they are so, so smart.

Meanwhile, you've done everything they told you to do. You did everything right, you saved, you sacrificed to have more savings later, paid your taxes and now you're left wondering if your retirement savings are secure.

You find yourself skating on thin ice and now the ice is cracking.

What can you do now?

This is depressing isn't it? But it doesn't have to be!

The only thing we know for sure is that when YOUR IRA or 401(k) balance takes a hit, no one will bail you out. Bailouts are only for the "too big to fail" guys, not us taxpayers. In fact, it's us taxpayers who provide the bailout and bonus money for these guys!

Boy, isn't that adding insult to injury??!!!

It's not fair. I know it's not fair. How can we ever win?

You've got to find yourself asking:

> What happened to my retirement savings?
> Where did it go?
> How can I get it back?
> How can I keep more of it protected for my retirement?
> How can I make sure it lasts as long as I do?
> Who can I trust?
> How can I rescue my retirement?

I hear this every day from people, and it is heartbreaking. How did this happen?

All you want is an even shot; a level playing field.

Let me explain what's going on using football.

Let's say the Wall Street Big Banks are a team in a football game. The Wall Street Bank team quarterback throws an interception, and that's bad. But then, that doesn't count, and they get the ball back like it never happened. Also, instead of the usual 4 downs, the Wall Street Bank team gets 8 downs, or 9 or 10 downs if they need it.

Then let's say that even with all of those unfair advantages over the other team, they somehow still manage to be losing because they are so bad. So then they have their buddies in Congress create a law stating that the other team's points don't count.

So regardless of how bad the Wall Street Bank team plays, they still end up crushing the other team.

Now here's the thing… we taxpayers… **WE are the other team!!!**

**So it's pretty obvious that we have to get out of this rigged game and rescue our retirement savings so they can last as long as we do… and beyond.**

And it won't be easy, because unlike the big banks, we have to play by the rules. We have to create our own bailout and retirement bonus money. And we can… doing it the right way… not the easy way… the right way.

To give you an example of how challenging this is, we recently had a couple come in for estate and retirement tax planning. The wife was a doctor and the husband was an engineer. These were two highly educated people and both were exceptional with details.

But they could not understand how to do this planning. They were overwhelmed, because they never had anyone explain both the problems and the solutions to them in English.

All their advisors ever talked about was selling them investments; not real planning that addresses the biggest problems.

Investing of course is important. Saving is important, but the key is keeping it protected and rescuing it from the tax and technical traps along the way.

They didn't know where to begin, but now they not only know where to begin, they understand the issues and they know where they want to end up and how to get there, by following the logical steps I gave them.

And that is what I am going to do in this program for you.

So where do you start?

Let's get rid of all this negative and depressing stuff so you can focus on positive steps you can take to change the outcome right now.

Retirement should include enjoyment. And you can't have enjoyment if you are constantly worrying about uncertainty, volatility, taxes, running out of money or your financial world spinning out of control.

To get rid of all the worry and uncertainty, you can't just brush it under the carpet. You have to address it. Otherwise it just stews and builds.

So, here is a list of things that you **cannot** control, so we get them behind us and move on.

## You cannot control:

## The Stock Market

Wall Street and Bank financial shenanigans, like:

- Market manipulation
- Corruption
- Fraud
- Bailouts

## Recession

I'd rather focus on what we can control, and then you will see magical, positive things happen. I've seen this transition happen to many people I have worked with and I want it to happen for you.

Recently a long time client came to see me, her husband had died and she came with her daughters.

I remember when she and her husband first came to see me. They were losing a fortune in their 401(k) due to the stock market crash and they were relying on that money for their retirement years.

Rather than dwell on the obvious negatives, like complaining about Wall Street and where did their money go, we focused on what we could do now with what they had, and we created a plan, like the one I'll be showing you.

Well, when she came to see me, after her husband died, she was so appreciative and relieved to know that everything we planned out happened *exactly* the way it was supposed to.

She had more than enough income for life through annuities she had set up because they decided that they no longer could handle the ups and downs of the stock market as they got closer to retirement.

She also received a ton of tax-free cash from life insurance they purchased. In addition, she was considering using some of that money to convert her IRA to a Roth IRA to provide even more tax-free money for her and her children after she dies.

There was not a dry eye in the room when she told us this story, knowing that she had financial security at her time of need.

She even followed up with a touching letter she sent me. The last sentence said it all. She wrote **"You made a difference at a time when there was very little to look forward to."**

Her retirement plan was **RESCUED!**

OK. So what CAN you control?

Only the most important items:

—The ones that will allow you to ignore all of the other nonsense and focus on what's in it for you.

## What can you control?

**Taxes**  You noticed that I did not put taxes on the list of items that you cannot control, and some of you might question that, saying Congress controls that, not us.

But I'm going to show you not only how much control you have over the taxes you pay, but how you can capitalize on the tax code and make it work FOR you... legally.

**Risk**  Yes, you can control risk—I saw an ad on TV from a financial institution that used the term "unexpected risk". Unexpected??? Are you kidding me!

Risk is not unexpected. In fact, you PLAN for it. That's why there is such a thing as insurance, and that should have a place in everyone's retirement plan.

So yes, you can control some risk, or at least the biggest risks facing your retirement savings. I'm not talking just about investment risk. There's tax risk, and financial advisor risk. These are all things you can control, if you take action and create a plan to address and eliminate these risks.

**Financial Advisors**  That is something else you can control. You pick your own financial advisors and the financial institutions that handle your money.

That can make a big difference in how much of your money you get to keep. It can eliminate some of the most costly mistakes due to bad advice and uneducated advisors.

Just by addressing these things you can control, you begin to turn all those negative feelings into positive action.

## Turning Uncertainty to Certainty

Back to football… or other sports for that matter. If a team is winning, they tend to go into a defensive position to defend their lead. They are usually not that concerned with scoring more points, they just don't want to make mistakes and lose their lead.

Like that football game, it's time to defend your lead. You've saved and built up your retirement savings account and now it's time to protect and defend it.

Where do you start? That's where it can be overwhelming.

It's like a 1,000 piece jigsaw puzzle. You give these to people you don't like, right? Then you watch them struggle. It's great because your gift can last for months tormenting them every day!

You open the box and you have all these pieces with no clue where to begin. It's really just a box of total confusion.

That's how many of us feel about rescuing our retirement savings. But you need to address this now and create a plan… a solution. If you don't have a plan, you get the government plan.

## So where and how do you get started?

Like that puzzle, you begin with one piece at a time – maybe the corner pieces or you begin with the borders.

When it comes to your retirement savings you start with the biggest pieces.

I am going to give you those pieces – the corners, the boarders and everything in between. And, as you continue, the magic happens. It's not really magic, it's momentum. You're on a roll. With each piece, it gets easier and the puzzle quickly begins to solve itself.

## Like that puzzle, rescuing your retirement is a process that begins with knowing where you want to end up.

Beginning with the end in mind:

With the puzzle, you see the picture on the box and you know what the solution looks like. You know where you want to end up.

Recently I read about the 75th anniversary of the classic *"Gone with the Wind"*. It took author Margaret Mitchell 10 years to complete the book, but what was interesting was that she wrote the last chapter FIRST. She had a plan and she began with the end in mind.

Right now I am going to give you that plan by showing you which pieces of the puzzle to tackle first.

I call the puzzle pieces:

# The 5 Silent Retirement Killers:

It is essential that you address each of these items now because there is a good chance that your retirement savings are at critical risk of being diminished, or even lost by these silent retirement killers.

You'll see what I mean. The hard part is opening the box and looking at all those puzzle pieces, but I am going to guide you through that and tell you which pieces to begin with.

## The 5 Silent Retirement Killers:

1. **Taxes**
2. **Risk**
3. **Saving Money**
4. **Uncertainty**
5. **Inactivity**

## 1. Taxes

The single biggest obstacle standing between you and your retirement money

## 2. Risk

There will be risk to do anything, but that risk can be contained and even eliminated with the right planning

## 3. Saving Money

Saving money? That's a retirement killer? I thought that was good? Don't they always say to keep saving? Yes, but most people do it in the wrong place and cost themselves even more money and taxes in the long run.

## 4. Uncertainty

Uncertainty guarantees failure. You don't know what to do so you throw in the towel and do nothing, and that results in the worst possible outcome… guaranteed.

## 5. Inactivity

Doing nothing – You are your own worst enemy. But this too is under your control.

These are the 5 silent retirement killers

**I call them silent retirement killers because you don't know these problems even exist.**

**They creep up on you and strangle your retirement savings without you knowing what happened… until it's too late, and the damage is done.**

But this is only part of the big message.

You **ALSO** need someone to guide you through all of this, who works only for you. You need a competent educated financial advisor.

When it comes to your retirement savings, you rarely if ever get a second chance to get it done right. That is why you need professional help here.

I can guarantee you that many of you watching are probably thinking that you've already addressed all of these issues, so you'll be ok. NOT TRUE!!! Otherwise I wouldn't be here.

I'm telling you that I know for sure that this is NOT the case – In fact, everyone, EVERYONE I sit down with thinks they have most of this covered, and I have never had a situation where at least one major item wasn't either omitted or done wrong.

Mistakes in these areas are costly and unforgiving. If you make a mistake with your retirement savings, most times it cannot be fixed and you can lose a fortune. You have one chance to get this right. The tax rules that surround your retirement savings can easily engulf them quickly with one wrong move.

That's why you need a plan to rescue your retirement from the 5 silent retirement killers. These are things that you absolutely CAN control once you begin to put the puzzle pieces together.

Having a plan can save you big money, the right way.

## The point of all of this is that you can win by NOT losing.

As I go through the 5 silent retirement killers I want you to have your antennas up so you can see how they can all be avoided.

I am here to help you keep more of the money you make

And of course… more of it TAX FREE… oh… and by the way Tax Free is always better!!!

That's the plan for today.

Coming up, we'll open the puzzle box and begin taking out the pieces, addressing and eliminating each of the 5 silent retirement killers.

# Part 2

## Key Points from Part TWO:

## Big Message: It's the TAXES!

Taxes will be the single biggest factor that separates people from their retirement dreams. But the amount of taxes you pay is STILL under your control.

There are ways to start moving your taxable money to tax-free territory and create your own tax-free "safety zone." This is how you can reduce the uncertainty of what future tax rates could do to your retirement savings.

How to get it done: Take advantage of the two huge tax breaks that create tax-free money for you and your loved ones:

**Roth IRAs**

**Life Insurance**

## Remember that Tax Free is always better!

OK. Let's review. You worked hard, made good financial decisions and now have a retirement account to show for it.

But then I told you that your retirement savings were at risk of being lost. However, it doesn't have to be that way because this is totally under your control.

It's time to RESCUE YOUR RETIREMENT!

Let's address the 5 silent retirement killers:

## The 5 Silent Retirement Killers:

### 1. Taxes
### 2. Risk
### 3. Saving Money
### 4. Uncertainty
### 5. Inactivity

And by the way, this list doesn't include the one major factor that can make or break any of these silent retirement killers:

Financial advisors without expertise
—We'll deal with this a little later.

The plan is to keep more of the money you make and keep more of it tax free.

## You need a plan to move your money from accounts that are forever taxed to accounts that are NEVER taxed.

Remember that tax free is always better!

What if I told you that I can show you how to control the single biggest expense in your life?

Think. Going back your whole life, what is your number one expense? Is it your home, college, medical bills? The one item you write the most checks for? The thing that costs you most—and don't say your kids... I can't help you with that one!

It's TAXES!

That's number one on my list of silent retirement killers.

## TAXES

Uncle Sam has a target on your retirement savings.

You know, from the day you get your first paycheck, you're paying taxes, you're writing a check to the government for the rest of your life, whether it's every week, every two weeks, every month, estimated taxes. And it never stops. And even after you're dead, they write the checks for you.

Did you ever stop to realize the maze of taxes we are all tangled up in?

> You get a job... which is great... then you pay income taxes on your wages.
>
> You spend some of that money... and you pay sales taxes.
>
> You invest money in property... you pay real estate taxes.
>
> You die... and you pay estate taxes... it never stops.

So you would think that you would make an effort to control your largest single lifetime expense.

But most people don't. Yet, most people can save thousands or even hundreds of thousands of dollars in taxes over their lifetime if they created a plan to address it.

Think about the time you spend saving much smaller amounts of money compared to taxes.

Cutting coupons, or checking the supermarket receipt. Even if you did catch an item once in a while, how much did it save you?

Checking the restaurant bill—same thing. Do you sit there after a meal and check every item on the bill… and see who had what? Then you look around and eyeball them… Jim had the shrimp cocktail.

Then you question the waitress, and she's usually right anyway.

There's rarely a big payoff there, but that is not what really mattered to you is it? Think about it.

Let's say you did catch a mistake and you were charged for a $10 appetizer you didn't order, you feel great… and in front of all those people who must be thinking that nothing gets past you?

They should only know that your retirement savings are in deep you know what because you haven't spent one minute checking that!

But at least they think you are amazing for finding that mistake on the bill. Now think about how great that made you feel?

Come on. Admit it. You know you are eating it up. You found it. They didn't. You get full credit. They all wish it was them. It feels fantastic especially since everyone was watching. Even the restaurant owner is impressed! People at other tables look over and wish you were checking their bill. You are the man!

Now think about how great you feel, and hold that thought—and this is all over saving 10 Bucks!

If this is the euphoria that comes with saving 10 bucks, then can you even imagine what you might feel if you saved 10 THOUSAND dollars, just by checking your retirement tax plan as well as you checked that restaurant bill?

Well, your tax bill IS the single biggest bill you will ever pay. But unlike the restaurant bill, the tax bill can be reduced or even eliminated if you just put in a little time and addressed this now.

You'll see that in many cases, the savings can be way more than even 10 thousand dollars. It's more likely in the hundreds of thousands in most cases. How would that make you feel?

If **NOT** addressed, taxes will consume your retirement savings.

Those of us who have saved the most are the best customers for Uncle Sam.

Taxes will be the single biggest factor that separates people from their retirement dreams.

But all of this is STILL under your control

Your retirement money will be taxed at some rate in the future. Probably at a much higher rate, just when you need the money the most, when you are not working and you are the most vulnerable.

And when it does get taxed, it will be taxed at the highest rates in the land… ordinary income tax rates. No special breaks here.

And given the sorry state of our country's finances, taxes will have to be higher.

What if I offered you a way to control your future tax bills so that you'll have the retirement of your dreams, instead of retirement nightmares?

You need to rescue your retirement savings by moving them from accounts that are forever taxed to accounts that are never taxed.

Sound familiar?

I've been saying that for years, but now it is more important than ever, because taxes will soon rise to the point that they can limit or even eliminate some of the best options.

I want you to visualize your retirement account. You see it? Well now look under the hood. Your retirement savings are infested with taxes! You need an exterminator!!

They are a sitting duck for taxes. There are trillions of dollars in retirement accounts and easy prey for the government. They love to tax things that are easy to get at. We can't move these accounts out of the country like the big companies do and not pay tax. We're not going to get any special deals or bailouts from Congress like the banks do.

## Our retirement savings are the low hanging fruit just waiting to be picked.

Your retirement balance is already part owned by Uncle Sam. We just don't know how much we'll owe when the time comes.

That's a big uncertainty, but we can deal with that right now. Right now you know what it will cost because we know what current tax rates are, and they are still at all time lows.

But, new taxes are already on the horizon.

Now is the time to create a plan to take advantage of the current low tax rates.

So what can you do now?

## Pay taxes!

WHAT!!!

What kind of show is this??? Anybody can pay more taxes!

That's right anybody can, but most people don't and they lose lots more later because they don't look at the long term big picture.

There are ways to start moving your taxable money to tax-free territory—from forever taxed to never taxed—consistently moving your retirement money and other taxable money to what I call "the safety zone" a tax-free reserve fund—your bailout fund!

The more you pile up in the safety zone, the more tax-free money you will build and the less you will be affected by tax risk and the uncertainty of what future tax rates could do to your retirement savings.

## Convert your IRA to a Roth IRA and start building a tax-free retirement.

Yes, that means paying taxes now, but at much lower tax rates **AND** a lower overall tax since the tax will be paid on a lower balance… today's balance… which you know.

At least you know the menu price. You know exactly how much it will cost today. That's one less thing to worry about.

Roth IRAs remove the uncertainty of what future taxes could do to your retirement income. That's the best way to get Uncle Sam out of your retirement savings for good. And remember, he's not even your real Uncle. You know that, right?

You need to take advantage of the tax code now. The Roth IRA is one of the best ways to build a lifetime of tax-free savings.

We had a client who was a teacher who built up $500,000 in his retirement account from contributing for over 30 years. He took my advice and converted those funds to a Roth IRA as soon as he could. Lots of his teacher buddies told him he was crazy to pay the taxes upfront to convert to the Roth. They weren't falling for that one.

That was over 12 years ago. Now that Roth IRA has grown to almost $2 million… all tax free!!! He's pretty happy!

If that growth remained in his IRA, he'd be looking at one heck of a tax bill now! He'd be looking at even higher future tax rates, if he withdraws later.

He super-charged his Roth IRA with the same information I'm sharing with you.

This is riddled with curveballs and you have to know what you are doing. You must do it right!

But once you have all the pieces, you can be a happy tax-free retiree like my school teacher. You simply need the instruction guide and the tools to get it done right. It's much easier than putting furniture together and your plan will last much, much longer.

At some point in the future when you or your heirs begin to withdraw this tax-free money, you'll be very happy that you won't **EVER** have to worry about taxes, because you paid for that upfront and at bargain prices.

And, with a Roth IRA, you'll never be forced to withdraw money and pay taxes after reaching age 70 ½ like you would with a traditional IRA or 401(k).

You can keep it growing tax free for the rest of your life without ever being forced to withdraw one dime of it.

That's not only tax free, but tax freedom!

I have been advising people to do this for years, and some people actually took my advice! Can you believe it! Some people actually did listen to me and now they are sitting pretty building tax-free money every day.

I love when clients come and see me who did Roth IRAs—the ones who listened.

They don't even remember paying the tax anymore. That's in the past. Now they only focus on the good things, positive things. THEY are in control, **NOT** the tax man!

Wouldn't YOU like to be in this position?… never having to worry about taxes or mandatory withdrawal rules for your retirement income.

What's the downside? You have to pay taxes now. Big deal.

When people ask you your tax rate on your retirement income, how good will it feel to say ZERO %! That's the downside—a zero percent tax rate in retirement, for paying tax at historically low bargain basement rates now.

I've also had clients that didn't convert.

Now they complain even when they make money in their IRA. How crazy is that? Imagine that… worrying about your account balance going up because of taxes!

They complain because every time they make money in their IRA, they know that eventually they will have to share it with IRS and they have NO IDEA how high taxes will be when they do.

Those menu prices haven't been printed yet. But as you know, in any restaurant, they never reprint menus because the prices went down! When you see new menus, it's because the prices went up.

The new tax menus will have higher prices. That's not what you want to look forward to in retirement.

More taxes means that you keep less when you need it the most. What kind of plan is that? It's a plan for disaster.

Roth IRAs can help create tax-free money when you need it most – in retirement.

You are going to love not worrying about taxes, ever.

That's a great rescue plan!

Let's switch gears to another way to eliminate huge taxes:

## LIFE INSURANCE

Just so you know, as I say on every program, I do not sell life insurance. I do not sell stocks, bonds, funds or annuities. I am a tax advisor and an educator.

And, as a tax advisor I am advising you to take advantage of the single biggest benefit in the tax code… and that is the tax exemption for life insurance.

You've heard me talk about the incredible leverage and tax-free benefits of life insurance, mainly for your heirs. And that payoff is big. You turn relatively small amounts of taxable money into a tax-free windfall for your family. They will end up with millions more than you ever had… all tax free.

It truly is the best tax leverage available under the tax code. But it is actually better than you think, especially if you are thinking, what's in it for me? Anyone thinking that?

In these volatile and uncertain times, you need to focus on investments that give you control, options, flexibility and certainty. AND you want to remove both stock market risk and tax risk. AND, you want a guarantee. AND, you want it all tax free.

That's a tall order, but you can get all of that with certain kinds of permanent life insurance.

Most people think of life insurance as something that pays off after you're dead. That's true. But what if I told you that you could have access to your life insurance during your lifetime, so you could use it for yourself?

You could begin moving large amounts of money from taxable accounts into a tax-free permanent life insurance policy. The money grows tax free inside the policy.

It's harder than ever today to make money on investments, so the last thing you want is to share any of your hard earned gains with the government. You don't have to, if those gains are earned within a life insurance policy. If your money is going to grow, it may as well grow tax free. Agreed?

You need to realize that life insurance is an investment, but better than your typical investment accounts because it's tax free. Oh and one more thing; life insurance comes with something else you can never get from the stock market… a guarantee.

But how much can you invest? That's up to you… and the tax rules. Believe it or not, this is an area where you might want to invest the maximum you can into the policy. If you are approaching retirement or already retired and looking to shelter more of your taxable money into a tax-free vehicle, this is the place for you.

But the mistake most people make at this stage of life, is trying pay the least for the policy. How can paying less be a mistake? Everyone wants a good deal?

Because this is an investment, not an expense.

If you were saving money in a bank account, would you want to put in the most or the least? Of course you'd want to put in the most, because this is your savings.

You should look at permanent life insurance the same way, except that the investment is tax free. So why would you keep money growing in a taxable account when it can be transferred to a tax-free investment?

If you have taxable IRA funds, you can in effect, convert your IRA to life insurance, paying tax now at low rates on distributions from your IRA and using that money to fund your life insurance investment.

That accomplishes two things:

> **(1) You reduce your future tax exposure in your IRA by taking distributions now, and,**
>
> **(2) You build up a tax-free source of retirement funds should you need them.**

If it turns out that you don't need to tap into your life insurance for retirement income, the life insurance benefit builds for your family, also income tax free. For most people, it will be estate tax free too depending on the estate tax exemption level.

This is truly the best leverage available – and it's all under your control.

Once again, I do not sell life insurance, but as a tax advisor I have to tell you that the tax exemption for life insurance is the single biggest benefit in the tax code. Make it part of your retirement savings plan, and your estate plan.

But remember, this area of your life is a little tricky. You must do it the right way to receive all the benefits I'm telling you about.

Now is the time to create a plan to rescue your retirement and move your money from accounts that are forever taxed to accounts that are never taxed. It's the taxes!

Those two big moves alone – Roth IRAs and life insurance can single-handedly remove most of the taxes you or your beneficiaries will ever have to pay. Pretty amazing isn't it?

And this is all under your control. And this is just the taxes, the first of the 5 silent retirement killers. Tax-free financial security is now easily within your reach.

Let's go back to our list:

## The 5 Silent Retirement Killers:

1. **Taxes**
2. **Risk**
3. **Saving Money**
4. **Uncertainty**
5. **Inactivity**

We've already dealt with the biggest piece of that retirement jigsaw puzzle… THE TAXES. And now you'll see how the other pieces you need to rescue your retirement will fall into place very quickly.

When we continue I'll go through the rest of the items on my list and you will really see the magic happen.

# Part 3

**Key Points from Part THREE:**

## Big Message: **You can control RISK –** both tax and stock market risk.

---

Using annuities can provide guaranteed income for life, and guaranteed tax-free income for life in a Roth IRA.

Don't save money in all the wrong places! The way to rescue your retirement is by intelligently spending money now to eliminate risk, create Roth IRAs and move taxable money to permanently tax-free territory.

Eliminate uncertainty: **Trust yourself** to create your plan to keep more of the money you make. No one will ever care more about your money than YOU!

Doing nothing is not an option. It's time to create your plan, so you don't end up with the government plan, which always means more taxes.

And, as I always say: Move your money from accounts that are forever taxed to *NEVER* taxed.

Now is the time take action!

# PART THREE

Ok. We're on a roll. We're on a mission to rescue your retirement from the 5 silent retirement killers, so let's keep the momentum going.

Once again… here is the list.

## The 5 Silent Retirement Killers:

1. **Taxes**
2. **Risk**
3. **Saving Money**
4. **Uncertainty**
5. **Inactivity**

We've dealt with the taxes, by taking advantage of the biggest tax-free benefits in the tax code, Roth conversions and life insurance.

Let's move on to retirement killer # 2:

## RISK

When most people think about risk, they think about losing money in the stock market. That's investment risk.

But the absolute biggest risk facing your retirement savings is future taxes, and we have already taken care of that piece of the puzzle.

Once you move your retirement funds to the tax-free safety zone, that money will be all yours, unaffected by taxes forever, and that benefit carries over to your beneficiaries too.

It's powerful.

But let's address investment risk too. As I said earlier, for the most part, you cannot rely on the stock market to guarantee your retirement goals.

You don't need that kind of worry and uncertainty in your life at this point. You need financial security. You need to know that your money will last as long as you do.

Maybe you should look into annuities? Again, I don't sell them, but they are one way to guarantee your retirement income.

Similar to life insurance, they come from an insurance company and that is the only place you can buy a guarantee. The stock market provides no such guarantee.

With an annuity you can turn your savings into a guaranteed stream of income for the rest of your life, no matter how long you live or how sick you get.

You cannot risk a market crash just before it's your time to retire. There is no rescue from that. As we've seen with some unfortunate retirees, they were not able to recover from the last market decline.

Now instead of golfing, they are working at the golf course, if they can even find that work. Instead of riding in a limo, they are driving the limo. Instead of relaxing in the back yard, they are doing the gardening in someone else's yard.

**It is essential that whoever is at the top of your family tree has financial security. If they don't have financial security, no one in the family does. You are all at risk.**

If your mom or dad needs financial help, because they lost money in the market, who is going to bail them out?

Do you want your children fighting over who has to help you?

You need to address this now.

Annuities are one way to do this. They can give you predictable income for the rest of your life and eliminate risk.

My mother did that and no matter what happens in the stock market she doesn't care. She gets her annuity checks every month for the rest of her life… guaranteed! No risk.

She's made life much easier for all of us. None of us ever have to worry about her financial security. What a great gift she has given us. Her biggest decisions now involve her social calendar!

There is nothing better as you get older than to eliminate risk and guarantee your retirement income. Annuities are something you might want to look into to get both.

You can even go one better. Do the Roth IRA and purchase the annuities in your Roth IRA, like I did.

Why?

**The only thing better than guaranteed income for life, is guaranteed TAX-FREE income for life.**

Annuities may not be for everyone and may only be a part of your overall plan to reduce risk. If you are considering this option, then make sure you do your homework and work only with a reliable company and a knowledgeable and trustworthy advisor.

Now we move on to retirement killer # 3:

You'll be shocked at this one!

## SAVING MONEY

What? Isn't saving money what retirement is all about? So how could saving money possibly kill my retirement plan?

Yes, saving money is essential to build your retirement savings, but saving in the wrong places can wipe that out. Saving money sounds like a virtue and usually it is. It's something we are all proud of.

How many of you just have to tell people what you spent on something? How much you saved!

Those big box stores that sell in large quantities love you! Have you ever really finished that 30 pound jar of nuts you bought? But you saved money. We love telling people about the deals we get.

But when it comes to your retirement savings, your first priority is to get it done right.

This is not the place to be saving money. One wrong move and you could trigger a **_HUGE_** tax bill.

In fact, it's the opposite. All the best moves you can make right now require you to SPEND money, not save money.

> Roth IRAs... you have to pay tax now... don't save money here.
>
> Life insurance... that costs money now... don't save money here either.

It also costs money to buy the guarantee of income for life with an annuity. But if this is something that is important to you, don't avoid it thinking you're saving money. You could be losing a boatload leaving it in the stock market.

This is the time to rescue your retirement and that means intelligently spending some money now, paying some tax now, and not doing so is a mistake.

Also, looking for free financial advice, which is everywhere, is a mistake.

Advisor and financial firm fees are another area that every financial article tells you to save on. But the cheapest advisor may cost you in the long run.

### You've got to get the best, most reliable advice possible and cost should not get in the way of that.

I know there is so much out there for free but you have to be careful. Really careful.

Take my advice:

## *"You can't afford "free"… it's too expensive."*

The best money you'll ever spend is the money you spend to get things done right, the first time!

Let's move to retirement killer # 4:

## Uncertainty

As I said, now the puzzle pieces are quickly falling into place and your retirement rescue is almost complete.

Here's what I mean. You see, we've already covered uncertainty without even knowing it. What are we uncertain about when it comes to our retirement savings?

| | |
|---|---|
| Taxes? | DONE! |
| Stock Market? | DONE! |
| Whether your money will last as long as you do? We just talked about that with annuities. | DONE! |
| Probably the biggest item to be uncertain about is who to believe and who to trust to guide you through the process. | DONE! |

What do you mean, DONE?

That's easy. Who do you trust? Yourself, of course!

## Trust yourself.

## No one will ever care about your money and your retirement more than you do.

The more reliable, objective and unbiased information you have access to, the easier this is. That's why we have Public Television!

And with this type of education, you'll be better prepared to find the right financial advisor for you.

Trust yourself to learn and make better informed decisions

Here's the surprise… it's YOU!

## You are the one who will rescue your retirement!

I am giving you the puzzle pieces, and YOU are putting them together. Nothing left to be uncertain about now!

Retirement killer # 5… and this one's the most deadly:

## Inactivity – Doing Nothing!

If you don't take action, you won't have a plan and you'll end up with the government plan, which includes lots of taxes for sure.

Doing nothing will be costly, as tax rates increase and opportunities expire.

For example, I talked about the tax benefits of life insurance.

But if you wait too long, you may no longer qualify or it's way more expensive because you're older. Unfortunately your medical history gets longer as you get older. So you may as well get it done now while you can. Right now you are as young as you'll ever be, and probably as healthy as ever too.

## I can guarantee you this; if you do nothing, something bad will happen, even if not in your lifetime, it could affect your loved ones.

Remember that the planning you do now benefits YOU first and your loved ones later.

If after all of this you are still not taking any action, then it probably means you really don't want to. Admit it.

That's like saying you want to lose weight, but you don't want to diet or exercise or give up candy, chocolate, potato chips or dessert?

How's that working for you?

If you truly want a secure financial future, it is imperative to take action.

Going back to that football game… even if you have the lead, you still have to take defensive action so you don't lose the game.

Don't waste this opportunity to rescue your retirement savings for yourself and your loved ones. Don't sit on the sidelines and just watch.

I've been talking about football so much in this program, but what is football anyway?

Football is 50,000 people who need exercise watching 22 who don't. They are just sitting on the sidelines.

It's time for action.

So what's the solution?

We've gone through my 5 silent retirement killers, but you still need to do everything right so that all of the pieces fit together properly.

As with any jigsaw puzzle, a missing piece stands out like a gaping hole and that could be a hole that your retirement falls through.

The better educated you are on these issues, the better questions you will ask and the better prepared you will be to rescue your retirement. You'll make better choices and know if you're working with the right advisor for you.

But this still comes down to you taking action, getting educated and making sure you have everything you need to complete your plan.

It's your money. Trust yourself!

No one will ever pay as much attention to these details as you.

YOU are the one who will be rescuing your retirement!

I know, I know, we all want a magic formula to fix everything, or a magician to go "poof" and make everything right. Unfortunately that's often how we get into the deepest trouble – trusting the wrong people, assuming things are handled when they aren't and not taking action.

So please educate yourself, really rescue yourself. And start right now!

That's why I'm on Public Television, where it's all about life-long learning. The most important thing is that YOU are educated. That YOU have the right tools so that you can make the right choices and rescue your retirement.

**Begin with the end in mind,** so you know what you want to accomplish.

Maybe this little exercise will help you get going:

> What do you want for your retirement?
>
> Clarity, or confusion?
>
> Do you want to say Oh Wow! Look what I did?
>
> Or say: Oh Crap! Look at what I did… or didn't do.
>
> Do you want to fulfill your dreams… or create nightmares?
>
> Do you want to cash monthly income checks… or cash weekly paychecks?
>
> Do you want the freedom to choose to work… or will you have no choice but to keep working?
>
> Would you like to play on the golf course… or work on the golf course?
>
> Do you want to pay less taxes… or more taxes?
>
> Do you want your plan or the government plan?
>
> Are you making the right moves with your IRA or are you building a savings account for Uncle Sam?

I've given you some of the most important items to take care of.

There are many more.

It would be great to blame someone else if this doesn't get done right. But this is all under your control.

You now have the puzzle pieces, the big picture and the plan

The clock is ticking. Like a football game, time is running out.

But now you know where to begin and how to get to the finish line.

Make sure you are moving your money from accounts that are forever taxed to accounts that are never taxed.

You've heard the horror stories, but you can have happy stories instead.

## Get started turning negatives to positives,

## Uncertainty to certainty,

## Reducing your tax bill,

## Working with better educated advisors,

## Eliminating risk, and

## Creating a plan of action to keep more of the money you make!

It's your call.

## It's time to rescue your retirement, and keep it that way!

–By Ed Slott, CPA
Copyright © 2012

# IRAs are Different

I call IRAs:

## "The Black Hole of Estate Planning"

## IRAs are different than all other assets.

Estate Planning is different for IRAs.

IRAs are distributed differently than all other assets both during life and after death.

### Here's why:

IRAs pass by contract (generally not by will).

IRAs have required minimum distributions (RMDs).

IRAs have their own set of complex distribution rules both during life and after death.

IRA distributions can incur tax penalties.

IRAs are highly taxed upon death or withdrawal.

IRAs are subject to double tax at death (estate and income tax, plus state versions of those taxes) in addition to IRS penalties that can apply to withdrawals made by the owner.

IRAs receive NO step-up in basis.

IRA investment gains receive no capital gains tax rates.

IRAs cannot be gifted to others or transferred to trusts during lifetime.

IRAs cannot change ownership during lifetime, like you can do with other assets when you create an estate plan. This would trigger an immediate and complete distribution and end the tax shelter.

IRAs cannot be owned jointly, like other property can be owned.

IRA equity cannot be tapped the way home equity can be tapped without triggering tax and potential IRS penalties.

The choice of your IRA beneficiary determines the ultimate future potential value of that IRA to beneficiaries.

Trusts named as IRA beneficiaries must qualify under specific IRS rules so that trust beneficiaries are eligible for stretch IRA tax benefits.

IRA beneficiaries may qualify for special tax breaks that are often missed.

IRAs have no principal and income concept. The entire IRA (principal and income) may be distributed to the income beneficiary of a trust leaving little or nothing to remainder trust beneficiaries. IRAs in a trust are all principal because under trust law, IRD (income in respect of a decedent) is principal in a trust and IRAs are IRD.

KEY POINT:

**IRAs require their own estate plans and then those estate plans must be integrated within the overall estate plan that includes all of your other assets.**

# The Amazing Stretch IRA

What is a stretch IRA?

It's not in the tax code.

It's just a name to explain how withdrawals have to be taken by your IRA beneficiary after you die. This is about inherited IRAs or inherited Roth IRAs.

Required minimum distributions (RMDs) on your traditional IRA begin during your lifetime, after age 70 ½. After you die, that does not stop. Your beneficiaries must continue to take RMDs.

But your beneficiaries are generally much younger. They are your children or grandchildren and that is who we are talking about when we talk about the STRETCH IRA.

When I use the term "non-spouse IRA beneficiaries", it's anyone but your spouse—children, grandchildren, life partner or friend. An inherited IRA or inherited Roth IRA means a non-spouse beneficiary

**The Stretch IRA is the ability of your beneficiary to extend distributions on his or her inherited IRA over his lifetime.**

The stretch IRA payout is based on IRS life expectancy tables.

Why is the Stretch IRA so good? Why should you want this?

It's not for you. It's for your beneficiaries—children, grandchildren, etc.

The younger the beneficiary, the bigger the tax benefit—due to the longer life expectancy. The longer the life expectancy, the longer the money can grow tax deferred or tax free for your beneficiaries.

For example:

> The life expectancy of a 50-year-old beneficiary is 34.2 years.
> That means only 2.9 % has to come out the first year.
>
> The life expectancy of a 20-year-old beneficiary is 63.0 years.
> That means only 1.6 % has to come out the first year.
>
> The life expectancy of a 1-year-old beneficiary is 81.6 years.
> That means only 1.2 % has to come out the first year.

The longer IRS has to wait for its money, the more your family keeps and builds.

If your beneficiary only has to withdraw about 2 or 3 % a year, and the inherited IRA is earning 5 or 6%, the account will continue to grow for most of their lives.

This will continue until your children reach their 70's – and even at that point only about 6% a year has to come out. And that goes up as they get older. But at that point if they are earning more than 6%, the inherited IRA you left them is still growing. That's the big advantage of the stretch IRA.

**The stretch IRA combines the power of tax deferral and time and that provides your beneficiaries with exponential tax-deferred growth for the rest of their lives.**

It's even more powerful with a Roth IRA. A stretch Roth IRA is as good as it gets. All the distributions are tax free for life.

The life expectancy factor is the number of years they can stretch it over. It's the minimum that has to be withdrawn each year. Your beneficiaries can always withdraw more if they wish. They are not restricted.

That can be good or bad.

**Know your beneficiaries:** Some will stretch, some will spend it all right away so you might want to make changes.

If you think you need to have some controls put on your beneficiaries, so that they stretch the inherited IRA over their lives as you intended, then you might want to look into naming a trust as your IRA or Roth IRA beneficiary. More on that topic later on.

The longer the funds stay in your family, the more growth you have. Money that is not eroded by taxes grows the fastest.

### How does my beneficiary get the stretch IRA?

Your beneficiaries can only get the advantage of the stretch IRA if you set it up for them.

How is that done? Easy. You simply need to name beneficiaries on your IRA beneficiary form. Under the tax rules, all you need to do is name a person as your IRA beneficiary and that beneficiary is guaranteed the stretch IRA.

### Every inherited IRA can be a stretch IRA, regardless of your age or your beneficiary's age.

It's easy, but most people don't get it.

Why? No one can find a beneficiary form and that means that they don't have a designated beneficiary.

That's another term you need to know: **Designated Beneficiary**

### Do your beneficiaries qualify as "Designated Beneficiaries"?

If not, this can force higher taxes that have to be paid more quickly after death.

Who is a "Designated Beneficiary" and why is this so important?

A designated beneficiary is simply a beneficiary with a life expectancy who is named on the IRA beneficiary form. The stretch IRA is only available to a designated beneficiary, like your child, grandchild or any person. Only a person has a life expectancy.

Not all beneficiaries are people, such as an estate, a trust or a charity. You generally never want to name your estate as your beneficiary because the stretch will be lost. But you might want to name a trust or a charity.

If you are charitably inclined, this is a good move since your IRA is loaded with taxes. Better to give the IRA than other property.

If you name a charity, the stretch doesn't matter. The charity gets the IRA money right away and will probably cash it out right away so they can use it. The charity pays no taxes anyway.

If you need to name a trust as your IRA beneficiary, then the trust must qualify under IRS tax rules so that your trust beneficiary may qualify for the stretch. This is often done incorrectly.

This is where you need to work with an advisor and an attorney who really know this area.

But if you name people (such as your children, grandchildren, a friend or any person) on your IRA beneficiary form, then they can be designated beneficiaries and get the stretch IRA.

## Back to the IRA beneficiary form

I said that most people cannot find it. It really is amazing.

I mention this in every program, every seminar, every book… and yet it is still an epidemic.

If there is no beneficiary form, then the stretch IRA benefit will almost always be lost for your beneficiaries.

What happens then?

They must take withdrawals much faster, and pay more tax sooner under the rules that apply when there is no designated beneficiary.

When there is no designated beneficiary, then post-death distributions depend on when the IRA owner died.

There are different rules if the IRA owner died either before or after the required beginning date (RBD). The RBD is after reaching age 70 ½.

## If there is no designated beneficiary, and:

If death was **before the RBD**—the inherited IRA must be withdrawn under the 5-year rule. The entire account balance must be emptied (withdrawn) by the end of the 5th year following the year of the IRA owner's death.

**The stretch IRA is lost because there is no designated beneficiary.**

## If there is no designated beneficiary, and:

If death was on or **after the RBD**—the inherited IRA must be withdrawn over the deceased IRA owner's remaining single life (had he or she lived).

The most you can get is about 15 years, as opposed to maybe 40 or 50 years of tax-deferred growth with a stretch IRA.

**The stretch IRA is lost because there is no designated beneficiary.**

## To guarantee the stretch IRA for your beneficiaries:

You must name them on your IRA beneficiary form.

You must name people (as opposed to a trust, charity or your estate).

And your beneficiaries must be able to find that form.

Get a copy of your IRA beneficiary form for EACH IRA you have and for every Roth IRA, every company plan, 401(k) or 403(b).

The IRA or plan beneficiary form is the most important document for you and your beneficiaries.

## It is amazing to think that the one document that:

Determines the ultimate future value of your IRA

How much it will be taxed

How soon it will be taxed

Is the main estate planning document for what may be your largest single asset – the money you worked for most of your working life

Is, in effect, the will for your IRA

Will guarantee the stretch IRA

Cannot be found by anyone in America anywhere!

This is amazing.

Even if you have it, it has to be up to date and have the right beneficiaries.

If your IRA beneficiary form is not current, not only might your beneficiaries not get the stretch IRA, they might not get ANY of the IRA. It could go to the wrong beneficiary or the tax may be owed sooner.

I see the family horror stories all the time.

A few years ago, a New York City teacher died and her husband was accidentally disinherited because the beneficiary form was not updated, after they were married – and that was over 50 years ago! This made headlines in New York since he lost $1 million dollars!

### Kennedy case – US Supreme Court (January 26, 2009)

The daughter was disinherited on a $402,000 401(k). Her father neglected to change the beneficiary form after his divorce. His ex-wife, (her mother) got the 401(k).

Beneficiary forms need to be updated and changed when you have changes in your life, what I call "life events."

Examples of life events are a birth, a death, a marriage, a divorce, you had a new grandchild, remarriage, a change in the tax laws, etc. This means that something changed and the beneficiary form probably needs to be updated.

Right now, make it a priority to locate every one of your IRA and company plan beneficiary forms for every retirement account you have. As you check your beneficiary forms, you might spot some bad beneficiaries and that can be corrected now.

### Examples of bad beneficiaries:

> Naming your estate
> A trust for the wrong reason
> An ex-spouse

Here's what you need to check on each of your IRA and Plan beneficiary forms:

### Have you named both Primary AND Contingent beneficiaries?

The primary beneficiary is the one who gets the money first. If the primary takes the money, the contingent doesn't matter anymore.

### What's a contingent beneficiary?

This is the next-in-line beneficiary who will receive the IRA if the primary beneficiary has died or disclaims his or her inheritance. The contingent beneficiary is important in any estate plan.

Many estate plans fail because there is no contingent beneficiary named on the beneficiary form.

You should name both primary and contingent beneficiaries.

The contingent beneficiary is essential to give your family post death planning flexibility, especially to take advantage of disclaimers in an era of changing estate tax rules.

> Example – you might name your spouse primary, children contingent

> Example – you might name your children primary, your grandchildren contingent

But you should have a copy of the most up-to-date form and your family needs to know where to find this. If they cannot find it, the beneficiary may revert to your estate and the stretch IRA will be lost.

This is NOT covered in your will! Everyone thinks someone else took care of this.

## Do you have more than one beneficiary?

Many people have multiple beneficiaries, for example, 3 children.

Make sure you make it clear how much each one gets, by stating a fraction – ½ each, – a percentage – 25% each –, or the word "equally" if that is what you wish. Now check that the shares add up to 100%.

## Do you have to name your children equally? No.

It doesn't have to be equal. That is up to you, but you must indicate that. Otherwise you are leaving this up to a court or family fight trying to figure out what you wanted, or some beneficiary getting much more than the others; or one beneficiary getting it all and your other children getting disinherited.

## Final Check:
## Are each of your beneficiaries named?

Can the beneficiary form be read?

Are there riders or attachments?

Are you missing anyone?

Check the IRA custodial document to see if it permits stretch distributions.

If it's a company plan, like a 401(k), most company plans will not permit stretch distributions to non-spouse plan beneficiaries but all plans must allow non-spouse beneficiaries to do a direct transfer to a properly-titled inherited IRA.

Make sure everyone knows where the beneficiary form can be found after you die.

Once you have all of these items done, make sure the most current version of your beneficiary form is on file at the bank, broker or other financial institution where you have your IRA money, or at the company, if this is a 401(k).

## Let's Review so far:

What is the stretch IRA?

> We are talking about an inherited IRA. This is an IRA inherited by anyone other than the spouse, for example: your children grandchildren, etc. Post-death payouts can be extended "stretched" over your beneficiaries' lives, if they are named on the IRA beneficiary form.

How do your beneficiaries get it?

> They must be named on the beneficiary form. You must have an IRA beneficiary form for every IRA or plan.

> They must qualify as designated beneficiaries.

Don't name your estate.

This is NOT covered in your will.

You can name a trust and still get the stretch, under special IRS rules.

Your beneficiary form must be up to date. Make changes when you have life events. The most current version must be on file with the financial institution.

It's a good idea that your financial advisors also have current copies of all of your beneficiary forms.

And your family MUST know where to find it, otherwise you've done nothing.

## OK. So now you know how to set things up to make sure that your beneficiaries can get the stretch IRA.

What can go wrong now?

Plenty. They can still blow it!

Even if you did everything right. You named your children clearly on your IRA beneficiary form. What can go wrong?

First thing they should do is TOUCH NOTHING until they are working with an advisor who specializes in this area. Most don't.

This is essential. This is where many inherited IRAs are lost.

Your beneficiaries need to know this inherited IRA is subject to a host of tax rules. If not followed, the stretch could not only be lost, but the entire inherited IRA could be subject to tax immediately and wipe out years of earnings and gains in your life.

## Setting Up the Stretch IRA

First things your beneficiaries should do:

Obtain copies of the death certificate (the financial institution that holds the IRA will probably ask for a copy).

Find copies of the beneficiary form.

Find IRA custodial agreements or plan documents (for plans) to see default provisions and other rules.

## What if there is no beneficiary (or the form cannot be found)?

What is the worst case scenario? The stretch might be lost.

Someone will always get the money, but who and at what cost?

But if that happens, first check the default provisions of the IRA custodial agreement. It could still save the stretch IRA.

If there is no designated beneficiary, the stretch is lost.

## Are the beneficiaries aware of special tax breaks?

These will be missed if no one asks.

The IRD (income in respect of a decedent) income tax deduction might be available to your beneficiaries if the IRA was subject to federal estate tax. Don't miss this!

401(k) plan beneficiaries may be able to take advantage of these lump-sum distribution tax breaks:

- Net Unrealized Appreciation (NUA) for company stock in the 401(k)

- 10-year averaging

For each of these lump-sum distribution benefits: If the plan participant would have qualified had he or she lived, then the beneficiaries qualify too.

Check to see if there was any basis [non-deductible IRA contributions or after tax funds in the 401(k)] in the inherited accounts. These funds can be withdrawn tax free.

## Big Beneficiary Mistakes!

Taking a Check
– A non-spouse beneficiary cannot do a rollover – this is a fatal error and cannot be fixed.

**A non-spouse IRA beneficiary cannot do an IRA rollover. Only a spouse can do that.**

This is the end of the inherited IRA and all the tax is owed.

Another mistake:
I get this question a lot:
When my son inherits my IRA, can he just roll it into his own IRA?

NO!!!

Putting the inherited IRA into their OWN IRA is a fatal error too!!!

Your beneficiary cannot make contributions to the inherited IRA.

### Titling of an Inherited IRA

The deceased IRA owner's name – YOUR name – must remain on the inherited IRA account and the account must indicate that it is an inherited IRA by using the word "beneficiary" or "beneficiary IRA" or "inherited IRA."

There is no set format as long as the deceased IRA owner's name remains on the account and it is clear that this is an inherited IRA.

**"John Smith, IRA (deceased 10/27/11) F/B/O John Smith, Jr., beneficiary"**

Beneficiaries should change the social security number on the account to their own social security number.

## Moving Inherited IRA funds – careful here – remember that a non-spouse beneficiary cannot do a rollover.

The non-spouse beneficiary can move an inherited IRA to another institution **only by trustee-to-trustee transfer.**

Beneficiaries must take required minimum distributions (RMDs) each year, even with an inherited Roth IRA. Not taking RMDs is a 50% penalty and it applies to beneficiaries too.

After you die, your beneficiaries must generally begin taking RMDs in the year after your death.

Your beneficiaries may even have to take RMDs IN the year of your death. If you didn't take the RMD, it is taken by the beneficiary, not the estate.

## Some more big mistakes that beneficiaries make:

One person (a beneficiary) told me that they were told by a CPA that once they inherited an IRA, they didn't have to begin taking RMDs until they were 70 ½. WRONG! That's a 50% Penalty.

Another beneficiary was told not to take RMDs because they were not yet age 59 ½. WRONG! That's a 50% Penalty.

The 10% early withdrawal penalty never ever applies to an inherited IRA. In fact, your beneficiaries will only get a penalty if they don't take the RMD.

How much do they have to take each year?

Look below at the Single Life Table (for inherited IRAs).

This table will be used by every designated beneficiary to calculate post-death required distributions. These life expectancies are based on the IRS Single Life Table for inherited IRAs, reproduced for you below:

# Single Life Expectancy Table (for Inherited IRAs)

(to be used for calculating post-death required distributions to beneficiaries)

**(From the April 2002 Final Regulations)**

| Age of IRA or Plan Beneficiary | Life Expectancy (in years) | Age of IRA or Plan Beneficiary | Life Expectancy (in years) | Age of IRA or Plan Beneficiary | Life Expectancy (in years) | Age of IRA or Plan Beneficiary | Life Expectancy (in years) |
|---|---|---|---|---|---|---|---|
| 0 | 82.4 | | | | | | |
| 1 | 81.6 | 31 | 52.4 | 61 | 24.4 | 91 | 5.2 |
| 2 | 80.6 | 32 | 51.4 | 62 | 23.5 | 92 | 4.9 |
| 3 | 79.7 | 33 | 50.4 | 63 | 22.7 | 93 | 4.6 |
| 4 | 78.7 | 34 | 49.4 | 64 | 21.8 | 94 | 4.3 |
| 5 | 77.7 | 35 | 48.5 | 65 | 21.0 | 95 | 4.1 |
| 6 | 76.7 | 36 | 47.5 | 66 | 20.2 | 96 | 3.8 |
| 7 | 75.8 | 37 | 46.5 | 67 | 19.4 | 97 | 3.6 |
| 8 | 74.8 | 38 | 45.6 | 68 | 18.6 | 98 | 3.4 |
| 9 | 73.8 | 39 | 44.6 | 69 | 17.8 | 99 | 3.1 |
| 10 | 72.8 | 40 | 43.6 | 70 | 17.0 | 100 | 2.9 |
| 11 | 71.8 | 41 | 42.7 | 71 | 16.3 | 101 | 2.7 |
| 12 | 70.8 | 42 | 41.7 | 72 | 15.5 | 102 | 2.5 |
| 13 | 69.9 | 43 | 40.7 | 73 | 14.8 | 103 | 2.3 |
| 14 | 68.9 | 44 | 39.8 | 74 | 14.1 | 104 | 2.1 |
| 15 | 67.9 | 45 | 38.8 | 75 | 13.4 | 105 | 1.9 |
| 16 | 66.9 | 46 | 37.9 | 76 | 12.7 | 106 | 1.7 |
| 17 | 66.0 | 47 | 37.0 | 77 | 12.1 | 107 | 1.5 |
| 18 | 65.0 | 48 | 36.0 | 78 | 11.4 | 108 | 1.4 |
| 19 | 64.0 | 49 | 35.1 | 79 | 10.8 | 109 | 1.2 |
| 20 | 63.0 | 50 | 34.2 | 80 | 10.2 | 110 | 1.1 |
| 21 | 62.1 | 51 | 33.3 | 81 | 9.7 | 111+ | 1.0 |
| 22 | 61.1 | 52 | 32.3 | 82 | 9.1 | | |
| 23 | 60.1 | 53 | 31.4 | 83 | 8.6 | | |
| 24 | 59.1 | 54 | 30.5 | 84 | 8.1 | | |
| 25 | 58.2 | 55 | 29.6 | 85 | 7.6 | | |
| 26 | 57.2 | 56 | 28.7 | 86 | 7.1 | | |
| 27 | 56.2 | 57 | 27.9 | 87 | 6.7 | | |
| 28 | 55.3 | 58 | 27.0 | 88 | 6.3 | | |
| 29 | 54.3 | 59 | 26.1 | 89 | 5.9 | | |
| 30 | 53.3 | 60 | 25.2 | 90 | 5.5 | | |

## Single Life Table (for inherited IRAs)

This table will be used by every designated beneficiary to calculate post-death required distributions. It will never be used by IRA owners to calculate lifetime-required distributions.

## Example:

Assume the named beneficiary on your IRA is your daughter who was age 39 when you died. She uses age 40 to look up her life expectancy because that is her age in her first distribution year – the year after death.

The life expectancy for a 40-year old from the IRS table is 43.6 years.

This means that she is entitled to spread required distributions over 43.6 years. She only has to withdraw 2.3% of the account the first year. She only needs to use the life expectancy table once. For each succeeding year, she subtracts one from the life expectancy.

For the next year she uses a factor of 42.6 years, then 41.6 years, then 40.6 years and so on until the original 43.6-year term has expired, unless she withdraws the IRA before that time. The beneficiary can always withdraw more than the required amount.

Once you have the life expectancy factor, you know the stretch period. Use the balance in the inherited IRA as of 12/31 of the prior year. Then divide the account balance by the life expectancy factor to determine the amount of the annual required minimum distribution.

## What if the beneficiary dies?

Contingent beneficiaries no longer matter. The inherited IRA now goes to the beneficiary's beneficiary – the successor beneficiary.

If the beneficiary dies before the 43.6-year term has expired (in this example) and there is still a balance in the IRA, then the beneficiary's beneficiary can continue the remaining years left on the original 43.6-year schedule.

It is important for every beneficiary to name a beneficiary as soon as they inherit so that there will be someone named to continue the schedule if the beneficiary dies early.

This will avoid probate and other related estate problems. If the beneficiary names a beneficiary, the remaining IRA balance will go directly to that beneficiary with no probate, claims or other legal obstacles.

## Splitting Inherited IRAs

Back to multiple beneficiaries:

General rule: Use the age of the oldest beneficiary for determining life expectancy and how long the inherited IRA can be stretched.

That might not matter much if children are close in age. But what if one of the beneficiaries is Aunt Matilda who is 100 years old and the other is your great grandchild Jane who is 1 year old?

The life expectancy of a 100 year old is only 2.9 years – as opposed to Jane's 81.6 year life expectancy. That's a huge difference.

Exception: IRAs can be split so that each designated beneficiary can use their own age to calculate the stretch IRA payout period.

If multiple beneficiaries inherit the account and each one wants to use their own life expectancy, the account must be split by 12/31 of the year after the account owner's death.

Or you can do that for them during your lifetime. That's your choice, but that's a lot of paperwork.

## IRA Trusts

**Should you name a trust as your IRA beneficiary, in order to make sure your beneficiaries get the benefit of the stretch IRA?**

The stretch IRA is great, but…
Will all my beneficiaries want to stretch the account?

You can force that if you wish by naming a trust as your IRA beneficiary.

Don't name a trust for tax reasons; you do it for post-death control reasons. You name a trust to make sure your beneficiaries don't squander the inherited IRA.

In fact, a trust can accelerate taxes at high trust tax rates if the inherited IRA funds are held in the trust and not distributed to the trust beneficiaries. Trust tax rates are the highest in the land.

**Caution:** You need to work with attorneys and financial advisors who have specialized knowledge in working with IRA trusts. I'm not talking about just setting them up, but knowing what to do after death. Ask your attorney and advisors now, so they can be a help to your loved ones. A trust is also a non-spouse beneficiary and the same basic inherited IRA rules apply.

Will the trust allow the trust beneficiaries to stretch the inherited IRA? It can, if it qualifies as a **"see-through trust."**

## Basic IRA trust qualifications for the stretch IRA when a trust is the IRA beneficiary:

1. Trust is valid under state law

2. Trust is irrevocable or becomes irrevocable upon the death

3. Beneficiaries of the trust are identifiable

4. Trustee of the trust must provide required trust documentation to the plan trustee, custodian or administrator no later than October 31st of the year following the year of the account owner's death

All of the trust's beneficiaries must be individuals, to get the stretch IRA through the trust.

Title the inherited IRA properly:
**John Jones, IRA, deceased (date of death), F/B/O The John Jones Trust**

File for a federal identification number for the trust if this has not already been done.

Whose life expectancy will be used to calculate RMDs when the trust is the beneficiary? In other words, what is stretch period?

That will depend on the kind of trust—a conduit trust or a discretionary trust. Your estate planning advisor should review these options with you.

The reason you want your IRA trust to qualify as a see-through trust, is to allow the oldest of the individual trust beneficiaries to be treated as if he or she were named directly.

This will allow the inherited IRA to be stretched over that person's life expectancy. If the trust does not qualify as a see-through trust, then the IRA will be treated as if there was no designated beneficiary and the stretch IRA will be lost.

It will be based on the rules that apply when you have no designated beneficiary for your IRA.

If any one of the trust beneficiaries is not a person (for example, an estate), then you do not have a designated beneficiary and the stretch will be lost.

There is a 50% penalty on any RMD not made to the trust.

## This is why you need expert help here

Here's a recap:

> The stretch IRA is amazing because your beneficiaries can extend distributions out for decades, keeping that IRA away from the tax man.

To get the stretch:

> Make sure your IRA beneficiary form is current.

Where are the beneficiary forms?

> Designated beneficiaries can only be people. Don't name your estate.

Once your Beneficiaries inherit:

Touch nothing

Find beneficiary forms

Don't take a check or roll it to the beneficiary's own IRA – fatal errors

Correct titling

Be careful moving the inherited IRA funds (a non-spouse beneficiary cannot do a rollover – it must be a direct transfer)

Beneficiaries must take RMDs

Splitting IRAs for multiple beneficiaries

Naming a trust to guarantee the stretch – but here you need professional advisors

Tell your beneficiaries:

### What you have

What types of accounts?

IRAs – includes SEP and SIMPLE IRAs

Company plans

401(k), 403(b), 457, Keogh

### Where everything is:

Even if you don't want them to know while you are living, leave them instructions. They need to know where all your retirement accounts are.

## Caution:

You need to be educated and so do your beneficiaries. Don't have your beneficiaries attempt any of this on their own. Make sure you have an advisor that knows what to do after death.

MOST DON'T–
Ask the hard questions.

Press your advisor now to see if he or she is a specialist in this area. You want to be able to have the advisor help pass the torch from you to loved ones.

Share this information with your beneficiaries NOW.

Your retirement savings can provide a legacy for your loved ones for the rest of their lives. Discuss all of this with a competent educated advisor, especially if you have built up significant balances in your taxable IRAs or 401(k)s.

Your retirement savings **has not yet been taxed** so it is still subject to many complex tax rules. If handled correctly by your beneficiaries, **it can continue to grow** tax deferred or even tax free for decades more.

You've spent a lifetime building it up, but it could be gone in minutes with one wrong move.

The Stretch IRA Really is **AMAZING!**

# Life Insurance for Life and Beyond

Why I am talking about life insurance?

Because life insurance may be the most underused strategy to protect large retirement balances from being decimated by the highest levels of taxation.

Who's most at risk? Those who have the largest IRAs or other tax-deferred savings accounts.

Just so you know…

I don't sell life insurance, so why should I care?

I don't sell stocks, bonds, funds, insurance or annuities.

I am a tax advisor, but it's about the taxes.

I also believe most people don't understand how life insurance works as an effective planning tool.

I don't sell it and I am no expert in exactly how the various life insurance contracts work. That's why there are life insurance professionals that you need to work with for all the details.

But I do know how life insurance can fix lots of money and retirement problems, and even create wealth, tax-free wealth!

And you know… I love tax free!

I only care about the end result—the benefits. I want you to know how powerful the end result is. I want to give you enough here so that you'll understand what life insurance tax planning can do for you and your family; both during your lifetime and after your death.

So why don't most people take advantage of life insurance?

Because every time you hear life insurance you tune out, or put it off. Most times when you hear about life insurance you are hearing about it from someone who sells it, so you feel like you are being sold rather than being advised.

They're just trying to sell me something … you think. So you avoid the meeting or the discussion. And you may be right. Maybe you feel that you are just being sold, so you don't see a benefit to you. But you could be wrong!

I want you to understand what's in it for you from an objective, unbiased tax benefit point of view.

Well now you're meeting with me, so let me tell you why I believe life insurance is the missing piece in most people's retirement and estate plans.

## The tax exemption for life insurance is the single biggest benefit in the tax code.

I don't even think life insurance professionals use it or appreciate enough. That's why they don't sell enough of this product.

I put this brief guide together for you in the hope that you will see how tax planning with life insurance provides powerful benefits. Then, hopefully you'll continue this conversation with your life insurance agent who can fill in the details.

But now when you meet with him or her, you'll have a better understanding of the benefits and what questions to ask. You'll definitely be more involved in the discussion, especially when it comes to your retirement.

First let's see what the problem is? And what the solutions are?

The good news is that taxes are generally money problems and life insurance puts tax-free money in your pocket, so most tax problems can easily be avoided with planning.

Here are both the problems and the solutions:

On two levels:

The problems that affect you – **during your lifetime**

AND

The problems that affect your beneficiaries – your family – **after your death**

Why would you care about a solution if you didn't think you had a problem? If you have retirement savings, you have a problem!

If you have taxable savings, you have a problem and so do your beneficiaries.

## Risk

Most people think of investment risk, as in the stock market. But when it comes to your retirement savings – especially taxable IRAs and 401(k)s – an even bigger risk is **tax risk**.

Many people think that simply having retirement savings is enough. It's not. **It's what you keep that counts, AFTER taxes**.

There's a mortgage on your tax-deferred retirement savings. Most of that is owed back to the government.

Future taxes could be 50% or 60% or more by the time you reach in for yours. That's not real money. The only real money is tax-free money: spendable money – where you keep it all.

Plus with IRAs and 401(k)s, you have to take required minimum distributions (RMDs) on that money after you reach age 70 ½ years old and you are forced to pay taxes on the government's schedule, not yours. That's the government plan.

That's not REAL money, since it is all subject to tax.

Are you wondering what future taxes will do to your retirement security?

You should be. You have actually caused the problem. Especially if you have done everything right. You saved, sacrificed and built a healthy retirement account—a 401(k) or IRA.

So… What's the problem with IRAs?

They are tax deferred, not tax free. With an IRA, SEP IRA, SIMPLE IRA, 401(k), 403(b) or any other type of tax-deferred retirement plan, you received your tax deduction upfront. Your retirement funds have grown tax deferred all these years.

So far, so good. You have done well. But there will be a day of reckoning. You'll owe income tax when you begin to withdraw, just when you need the money the most. How much tax? We don't know? That's the problem.

You won't know that until you need the money the most—in retirement—or after you die when your family inherits. This uncertainty keeps people up at night.

So that is the tax risk.

But there is another risk—market risk.

Your retirement savings and other investments, if invested in the stock market are also at risk of being lost to more Wall Street fraud and manipulation, or a market crash at the wrong time for you.

## Let's review up to this point:

Typical tax-deferred retirement savings like IRAs and 401(k)s are subject to 2 major risks:

Investment risk and tax risk.

Life insurance can be used to remove both of these risks

**Investment risk:**    With life insurance you get certainty – a guarantee.

You cannot get a guarantee in the stock market.

**Tax risk:**    You'll never pay income tax on this money.

You need to create a plan to move your money from accounts that are forever taxed to accounts that are never taxed. Life insurance is the best provision in the tax code to do that.

Wouldn't you sleep better at night if you knew your retirement savings were no longer subject to these risks?

But still, the benefits are misunderstood and not used enough in planning.

## So what are the benefits and exactly how would you use life insurance in your planning?

First, when I talk about life insurance I'm referring to permanent insurance. Even with permanent life insurance there are several options, so you need to speak with an insurance professional for those details.

I'm not talking about term insurance here, which is more for younger families looking to get the maximum death benefit for their money.

I am talking about permanent insurance – for those looking for retirement security and tax and estate protection.

As I've already told you, you have a tax problem especially if you have significant funds in taxable and tax-deferred accounts. Your family also will have a problem after you die if no planning is done and they inherit mostly taxable funds. They will be dealing with the tax issues too.

They may also be dealing with estate taxes, depending on the tax law when you die. That changes all the time so you need to plan for the worst case scenario, and hope for the best.

Your family will most likely have a liquidity problem if retirement funds and other assets have to be cashed in quickly to raise money after death for taxes and other post death expenses.

Money is often needed after death to resolve all kinds of issues besides taxes: family squabbles or family members wanting money quickly.

The last thing you want is for them to have a fire sale, especially if there is a family business or other valuable property in your estate.

You don't want your family wasting or cashing out retirement accounts or other valuable property prematurely because cash is needed quickly.

You need to do a liquidity test right now, so you can see if your family will have a cash problem after death. To gauge the problem I take clients through my own type of **liquidity analysis**, because most people are not liquid enough to avoid having their family start selling off investments, cashing in retirement accounts and triggering unnecessary taxes.

## What does my Liquidity Analysis do?

It shows you how much of your estate can be turned into cash quickly without triggering taxes or losing property value.

Cash is often needed after death. There could be state estate taxes, even if there are no federal estate taxes. There are always expenses and the IRA is the last account you would want to have to tap to pay those bills and taxes. IRAs are subject to both income and estate taxes, which could eat up lots of cash quickly.

## You can work on this with your advisor or accountant/CPA

Here's what I do for my clients:

> Make a list off all the assets you own, less liabilities, mortgages, loans, debts, etc. to get to your net worth.
>
> Code all your property as liquid or non-liquid.

By liquid I mean assets that can most easily and quickly be turned into cash, without triggering a tax or without some cost. When you have to pay any type of toll to get to your assets, those assets are NOT liquid. Liquid assets are basically cash.

Here's how to find out how liquid you are:

Do a fraction:

## Numerator

The numerator is liquid assets: basically cash

Cash, bank accounts etc.

Do not include IRAs or 401(k)s here. Sure they can be cashed in, but that will trigger a tax, so they are NOT liquid.

Include only assets that could be sold quickly without triggering a tax or other expenses, or without losing significant value—like a fire sale.

## Denominator

The ENTIRE value of your entire estate, including cash

Include all your assets—business interests, real estate.

Include all property owned in addition to the IRAs.

Now look at that percentage. For most people it's about 5% if that much. In other words most estates are 95% illiquid.

That's the problem, unless you actually do have a ton of cash available, which most people don't. Most people realize at this moment that they have a huge liquidity problem.

Now you know you have tax exposure, stock market risk and a liquidity problem.

## How can life insurance help?

Two ways:

> During your lifetime

> And… After your death

## Lifetime Benefits for You!

During your lifetime, you have the ability to reduce both stock market risk and tax risk, by moving your money from accounts that are forever taxed to accounts that are never taxed.

You can actually do that two ways:

Roth IRAs and Life Insurance

Both cost money now, but with life insurance, you'll be creating a bigger pot of tax-free money later on, when it's most needed.

It would be great if you could do both (Roth IRAs and life insurance) and turn your entire estate into a tax-free windfall both during your life and after death.

But the more powerful way is with life insurance. Again, I'm talking about permanent life insurance that has cash value. You can contribute more with life insurance than you can to a Roth.

With a Roth though, it's easier to access your money if you need it.

Roth IRAs are income tax free too, but they are part of your estate and are subject to estate taxes.

But Roth IRAs provide no additional death benefit as life insurance does. Life insurance comes with a guaranteed death benefit and that benefit, unlike a Roth IRA, can be set up to be estate tax free.

### So what can you do to remove both the stock market risk and the tax risk?

You can leverage your retirement savings. You can leverage your IRA.

If you have a large IRA, it may pay to draw it down now and pay tax on the distributions. Then use those distributions to invest in a permanent life insurance policy.

Tax rates are still at all time lows right now, so now would be the time to strike. Even if it cost you tax money, it still pays because you are lowering your tax exposure on your IRA.

After age 70 ½, mandatory withdrawals from the IRA must begin. Since the money will eventually have to be withdrawn anyway, it may as well be leveraged by using the money to pay the life insurance premiums. You are basically paying off the mortgage on your IRA early. This way, you never have to worry about tax risk. And the funds invested in your permanent life insurance policy are now growing tax and risk free.

You can have lifetime access to the cash value tax free if you need it for retirement. During your lifetime you can in effect turn your taxable IRA and other taxable savings into a tax-free savings vehicle.

It's really just like changing pockets from taxable accounts to tax-free accounts, except that now you also have a built in guaranteed death benefit for your family. It's generally judgment proof too.

If you have other taxable funds you might want to keep those protected from future taxes too.

Many people who are looking for places to shelter money from taxes, stock market risk and lawsuits are stuffing taxable money into permanent life insurance as a lifetime personal protected savings account. All the growth is tax free for life, and beyond.

## Post-Death Benefits for Your Family

If you don't need to tap into the funds during your lifetime, your beneficiaries are guaranteed a death benefit. The stock market has no such guarantee. Your family will now have guaranteed access to a ton of tax-free cash. Tax free means they keep every cent—no tax erosion here.

They will have tax-free cash to pay estate taxes if needed. To pay expenses, debts, and mortgages, all without triggering taxes or having to sell a family business or other valuable real estate or other property that could trigger taxes.

If they had to use your IRA to pay these bills, they would first have to pay income taxes and maybe estate taxes too, leaving very little to pay bills, or for them.

So don't sit there and admire your IRA like most people do.

Leverage it now.

Use it. Leverage it, or lose it to possible higher future taxes!

## Never underestimate the value of leveraging IRA money by using it to pay life insurance premiums.

The larger the estate, the higher the estate tax. Having enough insurance money available to cover the estimated estate tax will avoid having to invade the IRA to pay the tax.

## Some people might say:

## But the current estate tax exemption is now so much higher that there will probably be no estate tax.

That is not an option you can plan with. The estate tax exemption has been changing up and down and you cannot take that risk.

Anyway, what's the downside? If there is no estate tax, the beneficiaries will inherit more money and it will all be tax-free! That's the down side.

## But what if there is no estate tax?

## There are plenty of uses for life insurance even if there is no estate tax.

Use life insurance to replace stock market losses.

Life insurance can also be used to provide tax-free money for beneficiaries so that they do not have to withdraw amounts in excess of their required distributions on inherited IRAs.

This will keep their income taxes lower, since the excess IRA distributions would have been taxable. The money they use from life insurance is tax free. This allows them to stick with the stretch IRA schedule instead of depleting the IRA before its time.

This is even more powerful for a Roth IRA, since the Roth IRA is growing tax free. This allows inherited Roth IRAs to last longer and continue to grow tax free for beneficiaries.

Life insurance can also be used simply to create wealth.

Your family can easily end up with millions more than you ever had—all tax free!

That's why when I talk to clients I give them this scenario. First we find their net worth, like I said earlier; the entire value of your estate.

Then I ask:

If I could create a plan so that after you die, your family will end up with your entire net worth, or much more, would that be a good plan?

Yeah… where do I sign up for that? Who wouldn't want that?

Does that mean there were no taxes or other expenses that depleted the estate?

No, but we planned for that. And those items can be paid from the additional tax-free life insurance money, with plenty more left for your family.

That is how any family's assets can be leveraged with life insurance, to eliminate the effect of taxes and turn what was a taxable estate into a much larger tax-free estate.

Here are some other uses for life insurance planning:

If you have no retirement account, you can actually create one with life insurance and have death benefit protection too—all guaranteed, by moving other taxable money into your permanent life insurance policy. This provides a lifetime benefit for you.

Life insurance can be a pension alternative, providing beneficiaries a tax-free stream of cash for the rest of their lives, similar to the stretch IRA, except that the insurance is better than a stretch IRA because it's tax free.

Another benefit: Money solves a lot of problems and not all problems are money problems:

It can help in situations where families don't get along. And it's not usually your children; it's the ones they marry!

We had a case where one of the daughters would not even talk to the other 3 children. But mom had come to see me and decided to take out $500,000 of life insurance, naming the 4 children as equal beneficiaries. When mom died, it didn't matter that one of the daughters wasn't talking to the others. They all got their money quickly with no arguments, no fuss, no courts, no probate and no dealing with other family members.

Life insurance does not pass through a will. It is not subject to probate or income tax.

## To review:

This is the basic strategy. Turning taxable money into tax-free money using the tax exemption for life insurance.

Moving your money from accounts that are forever taxed to accounts that are never taxed.

As tax rates increase, tax free becomes more valuable.

Life insurance like Roth IRAs removes the uncertainty of what future tax hikes could do to your retirement savings.

But is it all good?

## What's the Downside?

You might not qualify. You might be too ill.

You can get annuities for that. Annuities also give you a guarantee of income for life.

You must commit to funding the policy. You need to have funds available to invest. But that is where your IRA and other taxable funds come in.

Life insurance is not for everyone.
Don't go broke. If you don't have enough assets, you probably also don't have a tax problem and then it might not be for you.

Maybe you only need enough to protect a young family in case of an early death.

The bottom line is that life insurance provides tax-free cash — **tax-free cash is always the best source of money and also solves lots of non-tax problems.**

This is all good but people make mistakes when it comes to life insurance planning and understanding life insurance.

## Here are the 5 most common life insurance mistakes:

(Again, I am referring only to permanent insurance — with cash value.)

### 1. Thinking that life insurance is a cost and not looking at it as an investment

A bank account is a good example. The more you invest, the more you'll have. Putting money in a bank account is not a cost, it's yours. It's an investment.

Think of permanent life insurance the same way. It's an investment.

## 2. Trying to pay the lowest amount for life insurance

Sounds good right?

Do you want to pay $1,000 or $10,000?

With permanent life insurance, the more you invest, the more you have protected from taxes.

## 3. Not understanding the benefits

For example:

Life insurance provides a tax-free payout after death.

Judgment Proof

Lifetime access to cash value – tax free.

It won't cause Social Security to be taxed and you won't lose tax benefits, such as exemptions, deductions and credits.

Life insurance can be exempt from estate tax.

With life insurance you get a guarantee. This removes stock market risk.

The government has restrictions on how much you can invest, but you generally want to put in the maximum you can.

## 4. Improper Ownership

Don't own it in your own name. Why would you?

Keep it out of your estate.

For estate tax purposes, you should not own your own policy. It should be owned by someone else or a trust.

One caveat though: If you don't own the policy (which is good for estate tax purposes), you may only have limited lifetime access to the cash value.

The life insurance premiums should be paid by the beneficiaries or by the trustee of an irrevocable life insurance trust so that the life insurance proceeds will be estate tax free.

## 5. Not knowing it's tax free

I don't know if this is a mistake or a misconception.

Still, people don't know that life insurance is tax free.

## Let's review:

**Risk** is a silent retirement killer.

Life insurance can eliminate both stock market and tax risk.

It can be used during life to create a tax-free retirement fund.

Life insurance is not only income tax free, it can be estate tax free too.

You can contribute almost unlimited sums to a permanent life insurance policy and have tax-free access to your cash value during life, without increasing your income.

And don't forget about the most basic life insurance benefit. Aside from the estate and retirement planning advantages, life insurance protects families when there is an early death.

It's hard enough to deal with the loss of a parent, but at least life insurance can provide the needed cash so that life can go on, without having to make any severe changes due to lost income.

Life insurance provides money for the family – tax-free money.

I never met anyone who didn't wish they had more life insurance, especially a widow.

I like to say that "Life insurance takes care of families without first going through the government."
—Ed Slott

You need to review all of these points with your life insurance professional who can fill in the details, but now you are much better informed and ready for the conversation. You'll actually enjoy your conversation with your life insurance agent! Can you believe it?

## Life insurance is not only the single biggest benefit in the tax code, but it is also the most cost effective way to protect a large IRA.

You need to have a discussion with a competent educated advisor that in addition to being a life insurance professional, has the specialized knowledge in retirement tax planning.

The coordination is essential, especially if you have built up significant balances in your taxable IRAs or 401(k)s.

## As tax rates increase, life insurance becomes more valuable than ever before.

New health care taxes are coming as well as higher tax rates. You can plan for that now. And if it doesn't happen, what's the downside? You and your family have sheltered that much more money, since it won't have to be used to pay taxes.

## Here are the most frequent questions I get about life insurance:

## If the tax exemption for life insurance is so good—won't government take it away?

No. Why?

It's a social reason. Why do you think our government encourages us to give money to charity? If you give to charity, you get a tax deduction. Why does the government want us to give so much money to charities?

So they don't have to; to remove the burden from them.

It's the same with life insurance. Our government wants us to take care of our families so they don't have to. They want us to take care of our families with our own money and private insurance company money, so that the government does not have to.

## What if I don't qualify for life insurance?

More people qualify than you think.

I've had very ill clients who qualified, so you never know until you try, so don't assume you won't qualify. Leave this to your life insurance professional to check for you.

## How can insurance companies do this?

People constantly ask me this because the benefit seems too good to be true. How can insurance companies stay in business paying out these huge sums of money, when you pay them so much less?

They have actuaries. Don't worry about them. We won't hold any benefits! It's in the numbers and a large pool of people.

Insurance companies are among the most solid financial institutions.

## Why doesn't everyone do this?

I don't know.

I also think that insurance is not sold properly so you look at it as a cost rather than an investment. Many people think they are buying something and don't see how it fits into a plan.

A good financial advisor or insurance professional can explain the planning aspects.

## Which is better—saving in an IRA or an insurance policy?

Life insurance, hands down.

Let's compare life insurance to tax-deferred retirement plans like IRAs and 401(k)s.

## If you compare life insurance to tax-deferred plans, life insurance has several advantages:

Life insurance provides a tax-free death benefit.

Life insurance cash value can be accessed tax and penalty free.

With an IRA, withdrawals can be heavily taxed, and you could incur penalties too.

With a traditional IRA, you are forced to withdraw and pay taxes after age 70 ½.

Life insurance provides an income tax-free death benefit. Estate tax free too, if owned properly.

With life insurance there is NO risk of future tax rates increasing.
—The Roth IRA provides this benefit too.

But…

Here's what you **DON'T** get with life insurance that you do get with an IRA or 401(k). You don't get a tax deduction. But a tax deduction these days is a trap because you'll pay much more later!

## Come on Ed—Are you working for the insurance companies?

No. I am here for you!

I'm telling you how to create and build tax-free wealth using the single biggest benefit in the tax code.

"Life insurance is the only legal way to print money."
–Ed Slott

So there you have it: The problems and the benefits – both to you **during your lifetime**, and for your family **after your death**.

## Bottom Line:

Don't just sit there and admire your IRA or 401(k).

If you have a large IRA, you have a tax problem. It's tax deferred. It's a sitting duck just waiting to be taxed.

Use it, Leverage it, or LOSE it to future taxes.

Do something now while the best options still exist.

Move your money from accounts that are forever taxed to accounts that are never taxed.

# Critical Items for Critical Moments

**This is a list of essential items you and your family need to be aware of. Where can they find these items when they need them?**

## Personal and Business Information

It's often we see clients who cannot find anything. They just have files of papers, scraps totally disorganized.

You don't want your family scurrying around looking for items under pressure when an illness hits or after death (when you can no longer help them). I've received calls from the hospital. That may be too late.

## Wired Stuff

We're in a wired world now and much of the critical information is online somewhere or even in "the cloud."

### Passwords:

1. Social network site passwords: Facebook, AOL, Twitter, etc.
   Do you want family members to have access to your personal email after you die? Now is the time to let them know.

2. Online bank passwords

3. Brokerage account passwords

4. Email passwords

5. Online Credit Card Passwords

6. Other online account passwords (e.g. PayPal, eBay)

7. PIN Numbers

8. Telephone passwords:
   There's so much information in our advanced telephones. Smart phones have lots of banking and investment info on them too. That's why people go crazy when they lose them.

9. Location where other valuables are stored, including who may access, any passwords or codes needed to enter.

## Banking and Investment Information:

1. Bank Name, Phone # and Location of Safe Deposit Box

2. List of all bank, brokerage and other investment accounts
   Bank statements and cancelled checks – online access
   Account Numbers: Many people have several linked accounts
   Who are the contact people there?

   Anyone at the bank in particular that is your contact person?
   What's their name and phone number?

   Investment advisor, CPA, Broker, Insurance professional?
   What's their contact info? Phone numbers, email, etc.

3. Retirement Accounts
   IRAs and Company plans
   Roth IRAs, SEP, SIMPLE IRAs
   401(k)s, 403(b)s, Roth 401(k)s, Roth 403(b)s, 457 plans, Roth 457 Plans, Thrift savings plans, Keogh Plans etc.
   Inherited Retirement Accounts, inherited Roth IRAs

4. Annuities – who are they payable to?

5. Municipal Bonds

6. Treasury Bonds and Notes: some people have these in drawers from family events; from births, graduations and weddings — and family may not know about them.

7. Stock options

## Beneficiary Forms — Where are these kept?

1. IRA beneficiary forms

2. Plan beneficiary forms

3. Annuity beneficiary forms

4. Transfer on Death or Payable on Death beneficiary forms

5. Life insurance beneficiary forms

6. IRA custodial agreements

7. Plan documents — Summary Plan Description

## Essential Documents:

These might not all apply to you, but some of these will apply to everyone. For example: a birth certificate. Everyone was born, I think?

1. Birth Certificate

2. Adoption Papers

3. Marriage Certificates

4. Death Certificates: Obviously you are alive, but you should have these from people you inherited assets from, so you know when you inherited and what the basis of the assets were. You'll need this info when you sell these assets.

5. Immigration and Naturalization Documents

6. Passports

7. Visas

## Estate Planning Documents and Medical Directives:

1. Wills

2. Trusts – including separate irrevocable life insurance trusts, other irrevocable trusts, IRA trusts, living trusts

3. Powers of Attorney

4. Health care proxies

5. HIPAA releases – Health Insurance Portability and Accountability Act of 1996 – to authorize the disclosure of your medical information

6. Other medical directives

7. Living wills

## Other Benefits:

1. Social Security Benefits

2. Veteran's Benefits

3. Military Information

4. Club membership benefits

5. Inheritances or funds in trusts

## Tax Returns:

1. Personal tax returns

2. Business tax returns

3. Business and Personal Financial Statements

4. Gift Tax Returns – there are lifetime exemptions that have to be kept track of, including basis information

5. Estate Tax Returns from people you have inherited from

Basis information – tax information that can provide valuable tax deduction information

## Agreements:

1. Business or partnership agreements

2. Business and personal contracts in force – are there provisions that have to be fulfilled; money owed or money due?

3. Copyrights or patents – some famous estates became worth much more after death because of copyrights

4. Accounts receivable – money owed to you, loans you've made, even family loans. I know of a client who included money loaned to her daughter in her will so it gets paid back after death, from her share of any inheritance.

5. Installment sales – you want your family knowing who owes you money; otherwise, it may never be collected.

6. Accounts payable – money you owe. You don't have to worry as much here. Anyone you owe money to, will find your family, but it's good to know anyway.

7. Credit card info: People have lots of credit cards. How much is owed?

## Property Information:

1. Deeds to real estate – homes, second homes, co-ops, condos

2. Mortgages

3. Lines of credit – balances on those

4. Vehicle titles, loan documents and location of vehicles – autos, boats, planes

5. Household furnishings

6. Family heirlooms – to avoid fights and squabbles later on

7. Collectibles, antiques, jewelry – again, to avoid any post death problems, and so people can find these items

8. Foreign property

9. Leases on property – how much might be owed?

## Post-Death Instructions:

1. Funeral instructions – prepaid funeral arrangements

2. Cremation or burial wishes

3. Cemetery plots

4. Beneficiary instructions

## Insurance:

1. Life insurance policies

2. Health insurance policies

3. Long-term care policies

## Marital Agreements:

1. Divorce or separation agreements

2. Prenuptial agreements

3. Postnuptial agreements

4. Spousal waivers of plan assets; this does not apply to IRAs

5. Civil Unions – same sex marital agreements (like a prenuptial agreement)

## Family Members:
**Your family tree – so you know who all the players are. This would be very helpful to anyone planning your estate.**

Spouse
Children

Parents

Grandparents

Grandchildren

Great Grandchildren

Partners (unmarried partners you want to provide for)

Friends

Other relatives

Special needs individuals you want to provide for

Prior Marriages – this list may be long for some!

Children of prior marriages

## Advisor Information:

Names and contact info, email, phone numbers, addresses

1. CPA

2. Financial Advisor

3. Insurance Agent

4. Attorney

5. Letter to beneficiaries detailing wishes/suggestions

6. Trustees of trusts

7. Executor or Administrator

## Names of other professionals and friends who might be helpful:

Names and contact info, email, phone numbers, addresses

Doctors

Clergy

Charities you care about

# 11 Ways to Supercharge Your Roth IRA

### Roth IRAs Build Tax-Free Retirement Savings

The goal is to build your retirement savings in a tax-free account. This is what I call moving your retirement savings from accounts that are forever taxed to accounts that are never taxed.

Roth conversions are available to everyone.

Some still think there are restrictions, but those were repealed and now everyone qualifies.

Roth IRAs come in 2 types:

Contributions and Conversions

### Roth IRA Contributions

Contributions are the $5,000 ($6,000 if 50 or over) annual contribution amounts for those who have earned income.

There are high income restrictions on who can contribute but those are easily by-passed. You can contribute to a nondeductible IRA and then convert it. You have to have earnings though to contribute to an IRA. While you cannot contribute to a traditional IRA after age 70 ½, you can contribute to a Roth IRA after age 70 ½.

## Roth IRA Conversions

The big money is in Roth conversions and you can convert unlimited amounts. Also, there is no income limit on who can convert.

Roth IRAs have no lifetime required minimum distributions (RMDs). You never have to take RMDs for the rest of your life. Your money just grows tax free, and you can pass your Roth IRA to a spouse who also does not have to take RMDs

RMDs don't begin until a non-spouse beneficiary inherits, like your children or grandchildren.

### How to decide if the Roth IRA is right for you

### Ask yourself these 3 questions:
When? What? Where?

1. When do you think you will need access to your money?

2. What do you think your future tax rate will be?

3. Where will you get the money from to pay the tax on the Roth conversion?

Not only can everyone convert, the amount you can convert is unlimited. Of course you have to pay taxes when you convert.

But given the historic low tax rates right now, this may be the best money you have ever spent moving your retirement funds to permanent tax-free territory.

## 11 Ways to Supercharge Your Roth IRA

**1. Contribute the maximum you can** $5,000 ($6,000 if age 50 or over)

You need earnings (from wages or self employment).

Even alimony qualifies as earnings. Who says you didn't earn it!

But child support payments do not count as earnings.

Combat pay counts as earnings, even though it may not be taxable.

Unemployment Insurance does NOT qualify as earnings.

Self-employed income counts too.

You can contribute to a Roth IRA at any age, even after age 70 ½. With a traditional IRA you can no longer contribute after age 70 ½. In fact, with a traditional IRA, you have to begin withdrawing and paying tax once you reach age 70 ½, whether you want to or not!

There is no risk with a Roth IRA contribution. If you need the money, you can withdraw your Roth contributions any time for any reason, tax and penalty free. Not the earnings or converted funds, but the Roth contributions.

If you are age 59 ½ or older, the converted funds can also be withdrawn tax and penalty free. You don't have to hold that money (the converted funds) for 5 years once you reach age 59 ½.

## 2. Capitalize on Low Tax Rates – Do a Roth Conversion

Get 'em while they last! Roth conversions that is – at low bargain basement prices. Taxes are as low as they will ever be. And it seems clear that future taxes will be higher.

Paying the tax now will avoid it later and your retirement money will be tax free for life. You'll actually be saving big money later by taking the tax hit now.

You'll have more tax-free money when you need it the most, in retirement, when you are no longer working and you'll need to keep more of your money protected from future taxes.

## 3. Roth Conversion Do-Over's can help you convert the optimum amount at the lowest tax rate

Roth IRA conversions come with a built in safety net, so risk can be eliminated.

It's called a Roth recharacterization. It means undoing your Roth conversion like it never happened. Everyone can do it and you don't need a reason. You get to evaluate your conversion decision with more information available to you.

When you first convert, there is uncertainty:

You are unsure of how much tax it will cost you.

You are unsure of your tax bracket for that year.
- you don't know your income for sure until the year ends
- bonuses
- losses
- tax deductions
- other income items

You are unsure of how your investments will perform.

You are unsure if you'll have the money to pay the tax.

You are unsure of any tax law changes that might take place.

**But you have until October 15th of the year after the conversion to recharacterize and by that time, these questions will be answered.**

You'll have all the information you need to make a better informed decision. You'll have more time to evaluate, and that is a big advantage.

You can convert the maximum, and, if your investments don't do well, you can recharacterize so you are not paying tax on value that no longer exists. It's like getting to bet on a horse after the race is over!

You have until October 15th of the year after the conversion to change your mind, for any reason at all.

So how can this super charge your Roth conversion?

You can take advantage of lower tax rates. By the time you have to make a decision, you'll know how much the conversion will cost you.

You can make sure that you are paying taxes at the lowest rates by keeping your conversion income in a low bracket, if you wish to. You can recharacterize enough to keep you from getting bumped to a higher tax bracket.

## 4. Re-convert

Use the cycle to your advantage

Here's how it works:

Conversion – Recharacterization – Re-conversion

Once a Roth recharacterization is done, those same funds can be re-converted, but you must wait until the later of:

1. The year after the conversion, or
2. More than 30 days after the recharacterization

What's in it for you?

You can maximize your options to lock in Roth IRA tax-free gains and pay tax at the lowest possible rates; also on the lowest possible balance.

Here are some examples of how the cycle works:

Rules on how soon a re-conversion can be done:

You must wait until the later of:

– The calendar year after the conversion, or

– More than 30 days after the recharacterization.


I'll give you a few examples here that span several years:

For a 2010 conversion – no more recharacterizations are available – the deadline was October 17, 2011.

If a 2010 conversion was recharacterized in 2011, a reconversion can be done after 30 days.

**Example:**    2010 conversion done in October 2010
Recharacterized September 20, 2011
It's the 30-day rule: These funds can be re-converted after October 30, 2011, and that will be a 2011 conversion.

**Example:** 2011 conversion done in April 2011
Recharacterized September 20, 2011
It's the next year rule: These funds cannot be re-converted until 2012, and that will be a 2012 conversion.

**Example:** 2011 conversion done in April 2011
Recharacterized January 10, 2012
It's the 30-day rule: These funds can be re-converted after February 10, 2012 and that will be a 2012 conversion.

**Example:** 2012 conversion done in April 2012
Recharacterized January 10, 2013
It's the 30-day rule: These funds can be re-converted after February 10, 2013 and that will be a 2013 conversion.

Other IRA or plan funds that still exist (that were not converted) have no conversion timing restrictions.

Hopefully you get the idea of how the cycle works.

Now I'm going to show you how to capitalize on this cycle.

## 5. Convert to Several New Roth IRAs

Use a **Multiple Account Strategy**. You can cherry-pick winners or losers.

If you convert everything to one Roth, you cannot cherry-pick and only get rid of the losers. You have to add in all the gains and losses.

### Better strategy: Consider converting to multiple Roth IRA accounts and keep only the accounts that do best.

Put different types of investments in different Roth IRAs

| **For example:** | Health care | Aggressive investments |
| --- | --- | --- |
| | Real estate | Utilities |
| | Conservative investments | |

Get rid of losers.

Does this mean you have to keep track of 5 or 6 different Roth IRAs?

Yes, but only until the time to recharacterize expires. Keep the separate Roth accounts until the deadline (the Oct. 15th date) to recharacterize expires. Then you can combine all your Roth IRAs into one master account again. This is lots of paperwork but worth it to give you every possible advantage using the tax code to supercharge your Roth IRA.

## 6. Have grandma convert and have her name her children or grandchildren as beneficiaries

Consider naming grandchildren as beneficiaries since they have a longer life expectancy and it can be worth more to them over time, especially when it is a tax-free Roth IRA.

Benefit to naming children:
-Longer life expectancy and no taxes for life

A 20-year-old has a 63 year life expectancy
$100,000 over 63.0 years at 8% = $2,511,000

A 10-year-old has a 72.8 year life expectancy
$100,000 over 72.8 years at 8% = $4,641,000

A 1-year-old has an 81.6 year life expectancy
$100,000 over 81.6 years at 8% = $8,167,000

All tax free for life! Imagine if someone ever did that for you.

You can gift grandma the money to convert. Make sure she names the right beneficiaries! YOU or your children (her grandchildren).

Benefit to naming you:
Say you are already in a high tax bracket.

Let's say you are an executive or professional in a high tax bracket. The last thing you need is to inherit a taxable IRA from your mom or dad.

But your mom or dad doesn't have the money to convert to a Roth. They need their money and it's not worth converting for them.

You can gift them the money to pay the tax on their Roth IRA conversions. You will inherit these funds as an inherited Roth IRA and will never have to pay tax on those funds.

In effect, you paid tax at your mom or dad's much lower tax rates, instead of what would have been your much higher rates. If you inherited and paid the tax, it would have been at your rates as you withdraw from an inherited traditional IRA.

Also, once grandma has a Roth IRA, she is no longer subject to RMDs, so if she does not need the money, it can keep growing tax free for her beneficiary – YOU!

### 7. Turn Required Distributions into Roth Conversions

IRAs are subject to required minimum distributions (RMDs) after reaching age 70 ½. Whether you want to take the money or not, you have to. But most people who are subject to RMDs don't need the money, so they just take the distribution and pay the tax.

### Those required amounts _CANNOT_ be converted.

People think they can because they are already paying the tax. It makes sense, but still, the law says you cannot convert required minimum distributions. That's why it might pay to convert before the year you turn age 70 ½.

**Example:** If you will turn age 70 ½ in 2013, then convert in 2012. If you convert everything, you'll never have to take required minimum distributions, because Roth IRA owners are exempt from lifetime RMDs.

But let's say you are already over age 70 ½ and subject to RMDs.

As long as you have to withdraw the funds anyway, you may as well use those funds to convert the rest of your traditional IRA funds to Roth IRAs.

### 8. Consistent Conversions

### Contrary to what many people think, a Roth conversion is not an all or nothing choice.

You can do partial conversions.

## Consider converting over many years to keep taxes lower.

Take advantage of our graduated tax rates:

$500,000 of income in one year generates more tax than $100,000 each year for 5 years, assuming tax rates stay relatively similar over that time.

## 9. Helping Your Children Create Roth IRAs

"Time is the greatest money making asset any individual can posses." – Ed Slott

And young people have it! Take advantage of it and see the exponential growth.

### You can make gifts to your children for both types of Roth IRAs

Make gifts to your children so they have money to convert their IRAs to Roth IRAs.

They might not have enough money to convert on their own – and would be wasting a major lifetime tax advantage. They are most likely in a low tax bracket and they likely have a much smaller IRA balance, so now is the time for them to convert. The lifetime growth will be tax free.

## Roth IRAs for children:

They need earned income to qualify for a Roth IRA contribution.

See if they can be put on books for legitimate work before the year ends (or get some holiday employment).

If they have earnings, they qualify for a Roth IRA contribution, and that can be made from funds gifted to them by you – their parent or their grandparents.

### Make gifts to children to create Roth IRAs or convert their IRAs to Roth IRAs.

What a great start you can give them!

## 10. Estate Tax Benefits

Roth IRA funds will not only pass income tax free to your loved ones, but most likely estate tax free too, depending on the amount of the estate tax exemption.

Your children are better off inheriting a Roth. If they inherit an IRA, they cannot convert that to a Roth IRA.

Inherited plan assets can only be converted by beneficiaries directly from the plan to an inherited Roth IRA.

## 11. Save the Roth for Last!

Roth IRA money is growing tax free, so let it grow! Leave it alone!

Tax fee money always grows the fastest because it is not eroded by taxes along the way… or ever.

Don't touch this golden tax-free fund.

Save the Roth Money for Last. Use other money first and let the Roth grow tax free. Why use money that's growing tax free when you can use other money?

# Extra – Don't mess this up now!

## Roth IRA Housekeeping

Now that you are supercharging your Roth IRA, you don't want anything getting in the way or ruining what you've created.

Make sure to name new beneficiaries once you open a new Roth IRA account or convert your IRA to a Roth IRA. You have created a new account and new accounts need new beneficiary forms.

The beneficiaries can be the same as the beneficiaries of your traditional IRA, if you wish.

Consider naming grandchildren as beneficiaries since they have a longer life expectancy and it can be worth more to them over time.

Move the money to the Roth the right way:

The best way is via a direct trustee-to-trustee transfer, where you don't touch the money in between.

If you are changing custodians at the same time as converting, most custodians require like-to-like transfers, so you may need to set up a new traditional IRA first and then convert once the money is at the new institution.

You can make a 60-day rollover to a Roth IRA as a conversion, but if you do, don't miss the deadline.

Make sure money went into the correct account—a Roth IRA account.

# Life Events

Life events mean that something in your life has changed. It might be big or small, but it should be evaluated to see what else changes as a result.

What kind of changes am I talking about?

Both personal and financial

For example, you had a birth, a death, a marriage, a divorce, an illness. These would be examples of changes in your personal life.

A tax law change, stock market decline, business or employment changes are examples of financial items that may require changes in your plans.

One thing is for sure, it is unlikely that a year would go by for most people without some change in their lives – personal or financial – and that means your plans need to be updated.

How will these life events affect any of your existing legal or retirement documents, like your will or beneficiary forms?

Too often we see people who have not updated their wills, beneficiary forms or other legal documents in years, even though some of the people that are in these documents may have died years ago. This is a common occurrence. This can give rise to costly legal and tax problems. Taxes and retirement issues could be affected.

Will there be tax benefits to take advantage of?

Will there be tax provisions you now have to comply with and should know about?

How will these changes affect your investing?

Your financial and tax advisors may need to be notified, as well as anyone involved in planning your estate.

**The point of this program is to alert you to assess the effect of any of these life events on your current plan.**

## Reacting to life events:

Evaluate what must be done.

Notify the proper people, advisors or financial institutions.

Then make any changes that are needed.

Make sure that your tax and retirement plans take these life events into account.

In addition to life events, you need to be aware of tax law changes that affect your planning.

Here are the more common life events that would probably call for changes in your planning, updating key documents and notifying advisors and family members.

### Birth or Adoption
New child, new grandchild

> That usually means that beneficiary forms need to be updated—your advisors or financial institutions should be notified.

> Setting up stretch IRAs to include the new child

> Wills need to be updated—notify your attorney or CPAs

> New dependents on your tax returns!—tell your CPA

> Look into life insurance—to provide for the child in case of your early death—notify your insurance professional

> Updating trusts if you have them—to include the new addition to your family. Some trusts already take this into account, but it's good to check anyway.

Maybe set up gifts to minor accounts – something to talk with your advisor about

Taking advantage of gift tax exemptions – putting money away for school

Maybe setting up education accounts

## Death

Again… beneficiary forms need to be updated to remove the deceased if he or she was a beneficiary.

This has been a problem – eaving deceased individuals on the IRA beneficiary form. The estate might end up the beneficiary. That would cause the loss of the stretch IRA benefit for children or other beneficiaries.

Contingent beneficiaries can become the beneficiary, if the beneficiary form was not updated after the death of the primary beneficiary. Your IRA, plan or life insurance money could go to an unintended beneficiary.

Wills need to be updated

Property records need updating

Estate tax returns may need to be filed

Keep track of date of death values – for step-up in basis if beneficiaries sell property

Life insurance proceeds need to be paid out.

Inherited IRAs need to be properly set up so that beneficiaries can take advantage of the stretch IRA.

Your beneficiaries should know about this and about the required minimum distribution rules so they take the right amounts each year and don't incur any penalties.

If the IRA or plan beneficiary is a spouse, there will probably be a spousal rollover that has to be done. This should be done as soon as possible. I have had more than a few cases where the second spouse died before the rollover was completed and it was a mess… and costly too. Tax benefits, like the stretch IRA were lost for the children.

## Marriage

This changes everything! As you probably already know.

Beneficiary forms and wills – for sure:

Notify your attorney and your financial advisor.

You probably want to name each other as beneficiaries – or not, depending on your situation.

There also might be a prenuptial agreement involved.

Taxes for sure – you will now probably file jointly

Property ownership will change as you might change some property to joint ownership and acquire property that you will own jointly.

Life insurance – that may be something you would want to have now that you have a spouse that you want to provide for.

## Non-traditional Marriage – same sex marriage

Planning is even more critical since the federal tax law does not offer the same tax benefits to these couples, even if the marriage is legal under state law.

**For example:**     No spousal rollovers

No joint tax returns

No legal protections automatically afforded to spouses

So beneficiary forms must be done perfectly and be kept up to date – wills too.

## Divorce

– Getting divorced

Make sure IRA and plan accounts are separated properly.

These days the retirement accounts are more valuable than some homes, especially homes with large mortgages or mortgages that exceed the current value. The home is not the bargaining chip it used to be when it comes to divorce. Now, it's the IRAs and other retirement accounts.

Beneficiary forms need updating

Property ownership needs to be revised

Wills need updating

- Already divorced
  Check beneficiary forms

- There have been too many cases where the retirement account went to the ex-spouse because the beneficiary form was not updated.

## Remarriage

Children from prior marriages that must be considered
Updating beneficiary forms
Prenuptial agreements

## Losing a Job, Retiring or Getting a Job (or changing to a new job)

6 Options for rollovers
You need to be advised on all your key Rollover Decisions

**Six Options:**
1. IRA rollover
2. Lump-sum distribution
3. Leave it in the company plan
4. Roll it to a new company plan
5. Roth conversion
6. In-plan Roth conversion

**For example:** Will you need income from your retirement savings?

Use the age 55 exemption from the 10% penalty—but to do that, you cannot do an IRA rollover, because this exception only applies to distributions from company plans, like your 401(k) plan, not from IRAs. You'll need to leave the money in your plan. To qualify for the age 55 exception, you need to have been separated from service in the year you turned age 55 or a later year. This exception only applies to distributions from plans, not from IRAs, so in this case, an IRA rollover would cause the loss of this benefit.

### Selling a House

Changing to a state that has different taxes – like NY to FLA, for example

### Health Issues:

– Getting sick

– Someone in your family getting sick

### Being Healthy:

That's the time to look into life insurance; while you are still healthy.

> Years ago I advised a client of mine with a large taxable IRA to get life insurance and create tax-free money for his family. But he wouldn't do it. He said he hated life insurance, but his wife who was healthy took the insurance. Turned out she died first and the children received $500,000 each, tax free. He then came back to me and said that **NOW** he wanted the life insurance but by this time he was too ill and no longer qualified.
>
> He died soon after and the children ended up using most of Mom's tax-free life insurance money to pay taxes on his estate which could have easily been avoided.
>
> ### Remember that the planning you do now benefits YOU first, and your loved ones later.

As you can see, most of these life events mean changing your plans and documents.

But to make it all work for your family, they have to know where everything is, before it's too late and your family ends up wasting thousands to figure it all out; not to mention unnecessary taxes. This is money that you worked for going down the drain.

Right now, could you find your IRA or 401(k) beneficiary form?

This is NOT covered in your will, as many people think.

Do you know where all your accounts are? How they are owned?

Do you know all of the items to look for?

Does your family know where to find the most important documents?

There is still time to answer these questions by taking action now.

Life events also include reaching certain ages

## Reaching Key Ages:

18 or 21 –   Children are no longer minors when they reach age 18 or 21 (depending on state law). They will now have access to funds in accounts that you might have set up for them.

50 –   Catch-up contributions can now be made to IRA, Roth IRA and company plans

55 –   The age 55 exception for penalty-free distributions from company plans

59 ½ –   The age where the 10% early withdrawal penalty no longer applies to IRA and plan distributions

Key ages for Social Security Benefits:
62, 65, 70

70 ½ –   Required Minimum Distributions must begin

## Let's review:

When you have changes or events in your life that change, take the following actions:

Assess the effect of any of these life events on your current plan

Evaluate what must be done

Notify the proper people, advisors or financial institutions

Then make any changes that are needed

Your plan should always be based on the most current information available – both personal information and financial information.

# Advisor Checkup

First things first: Do you have a financial advisor?

Do you have the ***right*** financial advisor for you?

Are you working with the right financial institution (your bank, broker or fund company)?

How would you know?
That's what we are going to find out right now.

When it comes to rescuing your retirement, you'll need the help of a financial advisor – the right advisor for you... or several advisors. They might specialize in different areas.

What can a financial advisor do for you?

They can guide you through the process of protecting your retirement savings from needless and excessive taxation. That's going to be a big deal when taxes increase as I believe they will, especially the taxes on your retirement savings.

An advisor can help you protect your retirement savings from risk and uncertainty, and help you keep more of the money you make. They can help you make sure it lasts as long as you do, and beyond.

Your retirement savings are loaded with taxes and you'll need guidance at some point, to avoid costly errors.

You might ask "Why do I need an advisor?" I already know where to invest. It's not how much you make, it's how much you keep, ***after*** taxes that counts.

In this program, I am not talking about making money. I am focusing on keeping it protected from taxes, especially future taxes, just when you need the money the most... in retirement.

You also might say… "Why do I need an advisor? I've got you!"

Yes, you do and you have all this great information.

"Ed – with all your books, DVDs, CDs, website and other items, you have provided me with a boatload of info – so I think I can take it from here and get this all done without an advisor."

No, you can't! This is too important, and most mistakes in this area cannot be fixed. They can cost you and your loved ones a fortune.

Yes, you have a ton of great, reliable, unbiased information from me, including this program. That is great, because the first thing you must do is educate yourself, so you can make the right choices, be better prepared, ask better questions and demand more from your financial advisor.

But you still need to find a competent, educated financial advisor to help you implement your plan, so you don't end up with the government plan.

I want you to use and benefit from this information, but with professional guidance.

I am providing this program:

    1. To educate you

    2. To help you get the most from your professional advisors and the financial institutions (banks, brokers, fund companies) that have your money. They need to measure up too. Having a big name financial company does not mean that you are working with someone who has been educated in this area.

This information is critical to you, so you can better evaluate the financial professionals you work with.

Medical analogy:

    Let's say you have a medical problem. So you do all your research and learn all you can so you can make better evaluations, understand the problem better and make better decisions; but you still need a doctor to do what's needed.

This is one of the most complex areas of the tax code and you have to know how to both comply and take advantage of the opportunities. That is where you need a professional or several of them, but they must have specialized knowledge.

There are lots of moving parts here. One mistake can be fatal to your retirement savings. When it comes to your retirement savings, you rarely, if ever, get a second chance to get it done right.

What if you already have an advisor or several advisors?

Then you should be using the education I am giving you here to make sure that they know what you need them to know to help you, and not hurt you.

Advisor mistakes are rampant.

I see this almost every day and it is heartbreaking, especially since most of these costly advisor mistakes could have been avoided if the advisor was better educated – and the consumer had more knowledge as well.

That's why you need to be educated with unbiased, objective, independent, untainted and accurate information like I am giving you here.

I don't sell stocks, bonds, funds, insurance, annuities, etc. I am a tax advisor and educator. That is why I brought my message to Public Television, where it's all about life-long learning.

**You have to be educated, so you can trust yourself and your own judgment when you receive advice.**

**No one will ever care about your money as much as you do.**

I am sickened over the horror stories I hear way too often. By horror stories, I mean when tax mistakes consume a retirement account. Or when poor planning means you and your family miss out on huge tax benefits in the tax code. These are costly and preventable mistakes. I am providing you with as much education as I can in this area so these things don't happen to you or your loved ones. You also need to be sure that your advisor is up to the task and does not make fatal errors when it comes to your retirement savings.

Your current advisors may be good at investing but they might not have the tax knowledge you need them to have to protect your retirement savings. This is a critical component.

Now that you have all of the information I have provided, you are ready to do an advisor checkup, of either your current advisors or new advisors that you are looking at.

Both current and prospective advisors need to go through this checkup. No one is exempt, even if they have been your advisor for years. They still need to be up to the task and now you have all the information you need to put them to the test.

**No one gets a free pass… your retirement savings are at stake!!!**

**No free passes!**

## You should demand more:

Here's a list of 5 demands for your financial advisor.

As I go through each of these, think about how your advisor stacks up:

**This is your advisor checkup!**

> **1. Education – specialized knowledge**
>
> **2. Loyalty – to YOU!**
>
> **3. Proactive planner – addressing items before mistakes happen**
>
> **4. Back-up plan – who does he or she rely on?**
>
> **5. Follow-up – especially AFTER the sale**

## 1. Education, education, education
### Education for your advisor or your financial institution is critical to you.

Think about this:

You are considering a major purchase. Think about what steps you would take to prepare yourself for a major purchase, such as a car, a major appliance or something that costs a lot of money for you – a major expense. You would probably take some time. You would get all the information you could (getting educated on the topic), look at comparative prices and options and other features.

Now you have all your research and information and you walk into the store, and within the first 10 seconds of talking with the salesman, you realize that you know more than him!

Has that ever happened to you? I can almost see you nodding in agreement.

It's happened to me. How does that make you feel? You're spending a lot of money. You want to work with someone who knows MORE than you, not less than you.

Well, wouldn't you agree that your retirement savings are a major purchase? This represents your life savings. This is money that you have worked for most of your life and you have one chance to get this right.

That's why you need an advisor that is educated in this area, and now you are raising the bar and demanding more from them when your level of knowledge is higher. The better educated you are, the better educated and more competent your advisor has to be to impress you.

You'll know in 10 seconds if your advisor has the required level of specialized knowledge. They better know their stuff to earn your business!

I am here for you – not them – so I am being tough on advisors for **your** benefit. And, because frankly, most advisors out there do not deserve your business!

I know because I train more advisors in this area than anyone in the country, and less than 1% of advisors take this training. Does yours?

That means that more than 99% of advisors might not have the knowledge you need them to have and you should not be working with them.

What kind of education should they have?

They should have specialized knowledge in tax and estate planning for your retirement savings. **NOT** sales training, but real specialized education in retirement account taxation. Remember that your retirement savings are loaded with taxes and taxes will be the single biggest factor that will separate you from your retirement savings.

Do they have the training?

Not sales training or persuasive technique training – using the right words or phrases to bait you and get you to buy what they are selling, even if it's not right for you. These are gimmicks used to disguise their lack of knowledge in this highly complex and specialized area.

Also, don't get sucked in by sales ads and gimmicks touting free advice. That cannot be good.

The biggest financial companies are running TV ads that say they have retirement specialists standing by to help you… for free!

Anybody who knows what you need them to know is not "standing by" waiting to give you free advice!

What happens when the free advisor gives you the wrong answer but you don't know it until it is too late? Who do you speak to then?

Low cost does not mean no cost.

It could cost you a fortune later in unnecessary and excessive taxes that probably could have been avoided, not to mention lost opportunities that could have turned your retirement savings into a tax-free windfall, for you and your family.

The better educated you are on these issues, the better questions you will ask and the better prepared you will be to rescue your retirement.

You'll make better choices and know if you're working with the right advisor for you. You'll know if the institution that has your money knows what they are doing. Most don't.

The biggest problem with many financial advisors is that they don't know that they don't know, and you and your family will pay the price.

Sorry to say, most people who call themselves financial advisors are really just salesmen and do not have the knowledge you need them to have to help you manage the taxes.

You need a specialist. This is a specialized area and one of the most complex areas of the tax code. Your current advisor might be able to make you money, but it's what you keep at the end of the game that counts **AFTER** taxes!

But here's the problem, and it's a BIG problem.

When you ask, everyone says that they know everything. Everyone says they are a specialist. I have never seen a time where the word "specialist" has been so overplayed, so much so that it has become meaningless.

The term is overused as much as the word "sale" in a store window. Have you ever noticed that in some stores they have a "sale" sign in the window – all the time? In fact, it's in the window so long, that the sign is faded. If everything is on sale all the time, what does it mean? Nothing.

It's the same with the word "specialist".

You see it in every ad – big full page ads from the biggest financial institutions say they have specialists all over the country, at every branch. How is that even possible???

Do you have any idea of the years of training it takes to be a specialist in this complex area of taxes and retirement planning?

I do!

I've been studying, advising and teaching in this area for over 25 years and there is still plenty to learn and the rules are constantly changing.

It's not simple and one size doesn't fit all.

What about credentials? Or what I call "alphabet soup."

It may look good, but these designations are getting out of control.

The Wall Street Journal recently ran a series of articles about these designations citing over 200 of them. Many of these are meaningless and more gimmicks than anything.

That's why we do not provide any credentials to advisors who train with us. They get education, not alphabet soup.

Here is an excerpt from one of those stories in The Wall Street Journal:

## The Wall Street Journal
## October 16, 2010

### Is Your Adviser Pumping Up His Credentials?
### Those Fancy Initials After Your Financial Adviser's Name Might Not Be As Impressive as They Seem
By JASON ZWEIG and MARY PILON

"Just when Americans seem more desperate than ever for trustworthy investment advice, financial advisers are brandishing a baffling array of new credentials – some of which can be earned with minimal or no study and a few hundred dollars."

"Increasingly, say regulators, financial advisers are using these dubious designations as marketing tools to win the trust of older, wealthier clients, in hopes of selling high-fee investments that aren't appropriate for them."

There are some solid designations of course which they did mention such as a CFA (Chartered Financial Analyst), CPA (Certified Public Accountant), and CFP (Certified Financial Planner).

Also:      CLUs – Chartered Life Underwriter
              ChFC – Chartered Financial Consultant
              These are professional designations in the insurance industry.

The Journal called most other designations "less rigorous" to put it nicely.

A serious designation is the first good sign, because it means they have something v aluable to lose – like a professional license – and certain standards need to be met and maintained. But even these advisors need to be educated in this complex specialized area.

## And...
## Steer clear of know-it-alls!

If they tell you they know everything about IRAs and 401(k)s, they've just told you that they know nothing.

When it comes to the taxes on your retirement savings – your single biggest lifetime expense, a specialist in this area should know that they don't know it all. Only a true specialist would know this. It shows they have a depth of knowledge so vast that they know they cannot ever know it all.

So what's the solution?

You should only work with competent, educated financial advisors who work for you and have the specialized knowledge required to advise you on each of these retirement and tax issues.

Check every advisor who wants to work with you. See if they have taken any real training in this area.

Your first loyalty is to you and your loved ones, not your brother-in-law or some other advisor who happens to be a nice guy.

A specialist in retirement tax planning should be taking extensive advanced education. They should be continually updating that education on a regular basis, since laws change so often.

**For example:**     Here is our training format for advisors:

In our basic foundation course – like basic training, we put advisors through two solid days of training. Additionally, they take many more days of advanced training through-out the year, if they choose to continue.

Advisors who train with us sit for several days, several times a year with us. We provide detailed course manuals that are up to 400 pages filled with updated technical material.

This is the most intensive and rigorous training available anywhere in the country in this area. Nothing even comes close.

Has your advisor ever sat through this kind of training?

Ask them to show you a recent course manual or book they read on the topic.

Tax laws are constantly changing. That's why advisors that we train are constantly returning to our programs throughout the year.

But most advisors do not take this kind of training and that is why I am warning you about this now.

Make sure your advisor is investing in this specialized education.

Demand more—this is your life savings!

**My rule:**

**If an advisor doesn't want to invest in his or her education, then you should not invest your retirement funds with them.**

They have to earn your business!

Most advisors will not like what I have just said… but that's OK.

I'm here for you… not them.

## 2. Loyalty—to YOU!

Whose side are they on? It better be yours.

You'll know by who pays them. That is who they are loyal to. You should be paying your advisor, so you know they work for you.

If they are working for free, you are still paying somewhere.

## You need to know that your advisor is doing what's best for you 100% of the time.

You'll need someone to guide you through all of this, who works only for you.

How can you tell?

What do they sell?

If they only have one or two products or strategies, that's probably what you'll get. That may not be a problem if that fits your needs.

A good advisor will always try to find the right product or strategy for you. He or she should not try to fit you into the one product he offers, if that is not what's best for you.

Advisors at some of the biggest financial institutions (banks, brokers and fund companies) are told to sell you products that earn the biggest fees for the companies. That is not good for you.

**For example:**     Fund company phone operators advise you to do IRA rollovers.

That is usually a good option, but it may not be the best option for you.

You need to know that there are five other options to consider, six options in all. But you won't get that from them, because they are paid to bring in IRA rollovers.

You need to be advised on all your key Rollover Decisions

**Six Options:**     1. IRA rollover
2. Lump-sum distribution
3. Leave it in the company plan
4. Roll it to a new company plan
5. Roth conversion
6. In-plan Roth conversion

If you are not paying them, they are not working for you! This means their loyalty is to their company, NOT YOU!

The result is often costly mistakes.

## For example:

A person I met at a recent Public Television seminar in St. Paul, Minnesota, told me that he saw one of the ads from the big financial institutions about rolling his retirement plan over to an IRA. Normally that is good advice, but the specialist on the 800# did not ask him two critical questions. (See below for the two questions).

They never do because they don't know, AND, they want you to roll your money over whether it is good for you or not.

He told me this after it was too late to fix this dreadful, costly mistake. Yes, he did a tax-free rollover, but when that money eventually gets withdrawn, when he needs it most, in retirement, he'll pay top dollar in taxes at the highest tax rates. He'll pay at ordinary income tax rates, and probably on a larger balance. The IRS is going to love this guy!

What if I told you he had the opportunity to pay less than half that amount at capital gains rates by not doing the IRA rollover?

He had that option but did not know it at the time. He realized it later after seeing one of my Public Television programs and getting the gifts offered on that program.

He told me that he probably could have saved over $200,000 in taxes if he got the right advice. This is horrendous. I felt terrible for him, but I could not fix the error.

Just so all of you know: The two questions that should have been asked were:

1. Do you have company stock in your 401(k) plan?

2. If yes, then what is the appreciation on that stock from the time it was purchased in your plan?

Only an advisor that is both educated and is providing advice based on your best interests would know to ask these key questions.

There is a huge tax benefit for what is called "Net Unrealized Appreciation" (NUA) in company stock in your 401(k) plan—stock of the company you are working for. By meeting certain technical tax rules, including taking a lump-sum distribution (as opposed to the IRA rollover), the appreciation on that stock can be taxed at long-term capital gain rates instead of much higher ordinary income tax rates.

But if these two questions are not asked, you would never know if you are eligible for the tax benefit, or how much the tax savings might be. The NUA tax benefit is forever lost however once the 401(k) funds are rolled over to an IRA. That is what happened to the person above, because he was not asked the right questions or given all the options.

When you are leaving a retirement plan, an IRA rollover is generally a good option, but you should know about the other five options as well. Each one must be considered and evaluated with a knowledgeable advisor… BEFORE you move your life savings!!!

This is serious business and you do need a specialist. Not someone given a title to make them appear to know more than they do.

Actually, at some companies, they actually do believe their people can be overnight specialists, because they don't know how much there is to know. Your biggest risk is that they don't know that they don't know.

The rollover option was best for the fund company but it is not best for every person. They weren't loyal. They were not giving their client the right options enabling him to tell which one was best for him.

Look at the financial crisis. Look at how much garbage was sold to the banks' own customers—worthless mortgage securities. Their customers lost a fortune. And at the same time, these big Wall Street institutions bet against them and made a fortune while selling their own customers down the river.

You need to know that your advisor, even if he or she is working for a big financial bank or firm, is loyal to you and only providing advice and products that are in your best interest – 100% of the time... NO EXCEPTIONS!!! – and of course – is educated as I talked about earlier – not in selling you stocks and other investments, but in tax planning for your retirement savings.

Ask tough questions and use your sixth sense to get an idea if you believe what they are saying. If your gut says no, then move on to an advisor that you are certain is working for you.

And this applies to family members who happen to be your advisors. They need to be checked too! Your first loyalty is to you and your loved ones, and your advisor should be loyal to you, even if his or her firm says otherwise.

## 3. Proactive Planner

Let me ask you something:

Would you rather have a problem solver or a problem finder?

You want a problem finder – someone who finds the problem and can fix it before it becomes a tax disaster you cannot fix.

That is how I train all of the financial advisors who attend our programs. I continually advise them to be proactive advisors and check things "before it hits the fan".

Your plan needs to include flexibility too, since tax laws are changing so rapidly.

To earn your business, your advisors should be advising you on a proactive basis. They should be contacting you when tax laws and planning options change and advising you when new opportunities are created.

When was the last time your advisor called you with this kind of proactive planning information? I'm talking about a call that was all about you, without trying to sell you something.

When was the last time your advisor checked your beneficiary forms? That is critical and is one of the most common and costly mistakes when it comes to your retirement savings.

**For example:**   Has your advisor been proactive in helping you plan out what happens after you die – setting plans in place now to guarantee a stretch IRA for your beneficiaries?

You need proactive planning from your advisor, but only an advisor who has the education and loyalty to you can provide this planning.

Now you are seeing how each of these advisor checkup points build on each other.

We have now covered 3 of my list of advisor demands – 3 advisor checkup points.

Let's continue to number 4:

## 4. Back-up plan

Who does your advisor turn to for retirement tax questions?

If they say they know it all, as I said earlier here, that means they have no clue of the depth of knowledge required in this critical area of protecting your retirement savings.

Your advisor should have no problem referring you to other advisors if he or she does not have the required knowledge in this area. That shows you that YOU come first and they have your best interests in mind.

Often other CPAs call me when they have specific IRA or retirement-related tax questions. They want to make sure that their clients get the right answers, even if they have to get them from outside experts.

Who does your advisor turn to for questions and back-up advice in this area? What if he or she is sick or is not available to answer questions? You need to know what the back-up plan is.

I used to get that question all the time from clients. "What happens if something happens to you? Who do I call?" It is important that you feel confident that your affairs will be handled if your advisor either is unavailable or does not have the expertise in the particular area.

What did I do?

I built networks of colleagues and other professionals including attorneys, other CPAs, financial advisors and other specialized advisors, so that my clients had back-up beyond me.

I was never worried about losing business to other advisors because my main concern was that my clients get the best advice, especially when that was not in my area of expertise. Your advisor should be able to do the same, even if they are a sole practitioner or have a smaller firm, like I did.

Not knowing everything is OK, as long as they have relationships with others that do.

They also have to be confident and secure enough to build a network of advisors and colleagues to work with that have expertise in all types of specialized areas, whether it is divorce, real estate, estate planning, trusts, charitable planning, special needs planning or other areas.

## 5. Follow-up AFTER the sale

You just made what might be one of the largest purchases of your life. You handed over your life savings – your retirement savings – to someone.

Follow-up after the sale is a critical point. This is the time when you need reassurance that you made the right decision when hiring this financial advisor.

### See how your advisor follows up and keeps in touch with you... *after* the sale.

Where is he or she now? Has he moved, changed locations?

That's OK. Did he notify you?

I worked with an attorney years ago and he moved to another state and did not tell his clients. He did estate planning, and when clients died, their family called me to find out where he was. No one should have to do that.

Just because you have hired an advisor, that does not mean you cannot fire him or her later. They have to continually earn your trust and be available even after the sale – in fact, especially after the sale.

Think about how great you feel after you bought something and the company calls you back after the sale. You want to be reassured that you made the right decision.

This is the time a good advisor will build their relationship with you.

Does your advisor know your family?

It's not only the knowledge, but relationships too. You want a relationship and a succession plan for your loved ones. You want someone to help pass the torch later.

We see advisors either go out of business or pick up and leave town, change locations or change companies. That's OK, but they need to follow-up with you. You need stability in your advisor.

We have been in the same location for over 30 years. We make an effort to meet the next generation so they are familiar with us, in order to have a smooth transition. Your advisor should do the same.

So there you have it.

## This is your advisor checkup!

## Your 5 demands — let's review them:

1. **Education — specialized knowledge**
2. **Loyalty — to YOU!**
3. **Proactive planner — addressing items before mistakes happen**
4. **Back-up plan — who does he or she rely on?**
5. **Follow-up — especially AFTER the sale**

This is your money. You worked for it. You need to DEMAND more from your financial advisor. He or she has to work for it too!

I've seen too many family horror stories and I am on a mission to match consumers with competent financial advisors.

# Your job is not to rescue your advisor; it's your advisor's job to rescue you!

Good luck—and do your advisor checkup!

For your reference:

Here is how to find advisors that have gone through our highest level of training. These advisors are members of *Ed Slott's Elite IRA Advisor Group*, an advanced education program focusing on tax and estate planning for retirement savings. You can find these advisors on our website at: www.irahelp.com.

They are not the only advisors to consider, but they have been exposed to my training and have access to our team of IRA experts when they have questions.

By Ed Slott, CPA

www.irahelp.com

Copyright © 2012